Black Lives Matter

Other Books of Related Interest

Opposing Viewpoints Series

Gun Violence
Identity Politics
Race in America
Reparations

At Issue Series

Civil Disobedience
Environmental Racism and Classism
Minorities and the Law
When Is Free Speech Hate Speech?

Current Controversies Series

The Confederate Flag
Gangs
Police Training and Excessive Force
Racial Profiling

"Congress shall make no law … abridging the freedom of speech, or of the press."

First Amendment to the US Constitution

The basic foundation of our democracy is the First Amendment guarantee of freedom of expression. The Opposing Viewpoints series is dedicated to the concept of this basic freedom and the idea that it is more important to practice it than to enshrine it.

OPPOSING
VIEWPOINTS®
SERIES

Black Lives Matter

Martin Gitlin, Book Editor

GREENHAVEN
PUBLISHING

Published in 2019 by Greenhaven Publishing, LLC
353 3rd Avenue, Suite 255, New York, NY 10010

Library of Congress Cataloging-in-Publication Data

Names: Gitlin, Marty, editor.
Title: Black lives matter / Martin Gitlin, editor.
Description: First edition. | New York : Greenhaven Publishing, 2018. |
  Series: Opposing viewpoints | Includes bibliographical references and
  index. | Audience: Grade 9 to 12.
Identifiers: LCCN 2017058634| ISBN 9781534502895 (library bound) | ISBN
  9781534502901 (pbk.)
Subjects: LCSH: Black lives matter movement. | African Americans—Civil
  rights. | United States—Race relations. | Racial profiling in law
  enforcement—United States. | African Americans—Social conditions—21st
  century. | Racism—United States.
Classification: LCC E185.615 .B543 2018 | DDC 323.1196/073—dc23
LC record available at https://lccn.loc.gov/2017058634

Manufactured in the United States of America

Website: http://greenhavenpublishing.com

Contents

Chapter 1: Do Black Lives Matter, or Do All Lives Matter?

Chapter 2: Does Black Lives Matter Have the Wrong Focus?

The Importance of Opposing Viewpoints

Perhaps every generation experiences a period in time in which the populace seems especially polarized, starkly divided on the important issues of the day and gravitating toward the far ends of the political spectrum and away from a consensus-facilitating middle ground. The world that today's students are growing up in and that they will soon enter into as active and engaged citizens is deeply fragmented in just this way. Issues relating to terrorism, immigration, women's rights, minority rights, race relations, health care, taxation, wealth and poverty, the environment, policing, military intervention, the proper role of government—in some ways, perennial issues that are freshly and uniquely urgent and vital with each new generation—are currently roiling the world.

If we are to foster a knowledgeable, responsible, active, and engaged citizenry among today's youth, we must provide them with the intellectual, interpretive, and critical-thinking tools and experience necessary to make sense of the world around them and of the all-important debates and arguments that inform it. After all, the outcome of these debates will in large measure determine the future course, prospects, and outcomes of the world and its peoples, particularly its youth. If they are to become successful members of society and productive and informed citizens, students need to learn how to evaluate the strengths and weaknesses of someone else's arguments, how to sift fact from opinion and fallacy, and how to test the relative merits and validity of their own opinions against the known facts and the best possible available information. The landmark series Opposing Viewpoints has been providing students with just such critical-thinking skills and exposure to the debates surrounding society's most urgent contemporary issues for many years, and it continues to serve this essential role with undiminished commitment, care, and rigor.

The key to the series's success in achieving its goal of sharpening students' critical-thinking and analytic skills resides in its title—

Opposing Viewpoints. In every intriguing, compelling, and engaging volume of this series, readers are presented with the widest possible spectrum of distinct viewpoints, expert opinions, and informed argumentation and commentary, supplied by some of today's leading academics, thinkers, analysts, politicians, policy makers, economists, activists, change agents, and advocates. Every opinion and argument anthologized here is presented objectively and accorded respect. There is no editorializing in any introductory text or in the arrangement and order of the pieces. No piece is included as a "straw man," an easy ideological target for cheap point-scoring. As wide and inclusive a range of viewpoints as possible is offered, with no privileging of one particular political ideology or cultural perspective over another. It is left to each individual reader to evaluate the relative merits of each argument—as he or she sees it, and with the use of ever-growing critical-thinking skills—and grapple with his or her own assumptions, beliefs, and perspectives to determine how convincing or successful any given argument is and how the reader's own stance on the issue may be modified or altered in response to it.

This process is facilitated and supported by volume, chapter, and selection introductions that provide readers with the essential context they need to begin engaging with the spotlighted issues, with the debates surrounding them, and with their own perhaps shifting or nascent opinions on them. In addition, guided reading and discussion questions encourage readers to determine the authors' point of view and purpose, interrogate and analyze the various arguments and their rhetoric and structure, evaluate the arguments' strengths and weaknesses, test their claims against available facts and evidence, judge the validity of the reasoning, and bring into clearer, sharper focus the reader's own beliefs and conclusions and how they may differ from or align with those in the collection or those of their classmates.

Research has shown that reading comprehension skills improve dramatically when students are provided with compelling, intriguing, and relevant "discussable" texts. The subject matter of these collections could not be more compelling, intriguing, or urgently relevant to today's students and the world they are poised to inherit. The anthologized articles and the reading and discussion questions that are included with them also provide the basis for stimulating, lively, and passionate classroom debates. Students who are compelled to anticipate objections to their own argument and identify the flaws in those of an opponent read more carefully, think more critically, and steep themselves in relevant context, facts, and information more thoroughly. In short, using discussable text of the kind provided by every single volume in the Opposing Viewpoints series encourages close reading, facilitates reading comprehension, fosters research, strengthens critical thinking, and greatly enlivens and energizes classroom discussion and participation. The entire learning process is deepened, extended, and strengthened.

For all of these reasons, Opposing Viewpoints continues to be exactly the right resource at exactly the right time—when we most need to provide readers with the critical-thinking tools and skills that will not only serve them well in school but also in their careers and their daily lives as decision-making family members, community members, and citizens. This series encourages respectful engagement with and analysis of opposing viewpoints and fosters a resulting increase in the strength and rigor of one's own opinions and stances. As such, it helps make readers "future ready," and that readiness will pay rich dividends for the readers themselves, for the citizenry, for our society, and for the world at large.

Introduction

> *"Kindness and compassion expressed by these two sides … that makes a big difference. Sometimes people just want acknowledgment."*
>
> *—President Barack Obama to* Time *magazine on the relationship between law enforcement and Black Lives Matter, June 2016*

A verbal reflex often emanates from those that either do not understand the Black Lives Matter movement or do not align intellectually or emotionally with its cause. That is, they reply to its mere mention of the group with the now-familiar refrain, "All lives matter."

That is indeed true. All lives *do* matter. Those that support Black Lives Matter are in full agreement. But that is the crux of the issue. The very assumption that all other lives matter is exactly why Black Lives Matter sprung into existence. The treatment of African Americans throughout the history of the United States, specifically by some in law enforcement today, strongly indicates a disparity between how the value of black lives is perceived compared to that of the white population.

One poignant scene from legendary, revolutionary television sitcom *All in the Family* from the early 1970s captured that difference in perception when racist lead character Archie Bunker referred to a young, black repairman as "boy." The worker responded coolly, but angrily, that he was not a boy, but a man. Bunker shrugged off the criticism, stating that he, too, was a man and never made a point of it. "You never had to make a point of it," replied the black man.

That "point" is why Black Lives Matter organized. It espouses itself as a global network with a mission to build local power among African Americans and serve as a force against violence inflicted against those in their communities. The chapter-based group considers itself liberators who seek an inclusive and expansive movement. It seeks to fight the nationalism it sees as prevalent in black America.

Indeed, making a point of it is the driving force behind Black Lives Matter. It understands that the civil rights movement brought legal equality decades ago, but that equality in the hearts and minds of Americans, especially those who wear police badges, has yet to be achieved.

That is where the debate begins. Some claim that little or no bias exists among law enforcement officials. They tend to believe that higher crime and incarceration rates among inner-city black males prove that they bring upon themselves any relationship problems with police. They furthermore argue that gang violence in inner cities naturally makes law enforcement officers warier of confrontations in such communities. Those against Black Lives Matter contend that justified fearfulness, not prejudice, has led to trigger-happy cops and unfortunate killings.

Black Lives Matter and its supporters assert that one need look no further than videos of such conflicts to understand what they see as truth. Whether recorded on police dashcam or by curious bystanders, their similarities are striking. They show police shooting unarmed black men who are either running away, pushed up against a car, or sitting unthreateningly inside a vehicle. One can argue that, even if an officer has been traumatized by previous racially charged encounters, he or she was not being threatened and that the only logical explanation is racism and a belief that black lives are more disposable than white lives.

Some cite statistics that indicate such is not the case. Many have asserted that most shootings involving citizens and the police have left white people dead. The numbers seemingly give ammunition to those who seek to weaken the arguments regarding police bias made by Black Lives Matter. Its detractors claim that BLM spotlights the deaths of African Americans at the hands of the police while ignoring those of white citizens. But the disproportionate fatalities—the fact that the percentage of black people killed by law enforcement officials is far higher than the percentage of the total number of blacks among the US population—adds fuel to the fire of BLM and its supporters. Black males ages 15-34 have been particularly and literally targeted. They were nine times more likely to be killed by law enforcement officers than any other Americans in 2016 and four times more likely than whites of the same age group. The kill rate among all black people in 2016 more than doubled that of whites and Hispanics.

Much gray area exists in exploring where the blame lies in such disturbing numbers, leading to many debates about Black Lives Matter. Among them is the very issue of African American gang warfare and interrelated so-called black-on-black crime. Critics claim that BLM should focus far more on creating solutions to those issues, which plague inner cities—most notoriously Chicago—and cause massive incarceration and far more deaths than battles with law enforcement. Indeed, the homicide rate in American inner cities remains alarming. Battles between rival gangs for turf and drug money have left thousands dead.

But the claim that Black Lives Matter is unfeeling and unresponsive to such tragedies can be debated. Supporters allude to efforts of Black Lives Matter indeed intervening in the disturbing gang violence that continues to plague major cities throughout the United States. Such work has been greatly unpublicized, perhaps because dramatic confrontations with police make for significantly higher television ratings and broader readership.

Another issue revolves around Black Lives Matter involvement in protesting right-wing speakers on college campuses. Critics, some say exaggeratingly, argue that the group seeks to limit free speech in a nation that embraces it. They voice their opinion that

Black Lives Matter works to silence opposition. But supporters claim that BLM efforts to prevent speakers from voicing their views are indeed overblown. They cite opposition from campus organizations and students that simply do not want far-right views espoused in their midst as more vocal than Black Lives Matter. And they argue that radical white supremacists simply should not be given a forum to express what can be dangerous opinions. After all, how many lives might have been spared had Adolf Hitler and his Nazi Party remained banned from Germany in the 1920s and early 1930s? Supporters of BLM state that it has every right to demand that white supremacist rhetoric remains unuttered in public.

Black Lives Matter is arguably the most controversial American organization to spring up in the twenty-first century. Many white people and, even some African Americans, feel threatened by its stated purpose and rhetoric. The most ardent of its critics contend that it worsens race relations in the United States by driving a wedge between whites and blacks and between police and the African-American community. They cite incidents of random murders of police officers by black men in recent years as evidence of deteriorating relationships supposedly exacerbated by Black Lives Matter. The result has been the "Blue Lives Matter" movement that shines a spotlight on the value of law enforcement officers and maintaining their safety. Even mild critics have offered that BLM should take a softer tone to improve relations with police.

The other side has praised BLM for its vigilance. Though no rational backer of BLM supports revenge killing of police, many claim that African Americans have been pushed to the limit emotionally by the spate of killings of its unarmed brothers by police and that physical demonstrations of anger have been justified. They assert that only through a show of force will law enforcement agencies be motivated to weed out proven racist officers and take steps to work with black inner-city communities as helpers rather than adversaries, thereby truly emerging as public servants.

Opposing Viewpoints: Black Lives Matter examines all issues pertinent to the organization in four chapters titled "Do Black

Lives Matter, or Do All Lives Matter?" "Does Black Lives Matter Have the Wrong Focus?," "Black Lives Matter: Peaceful Protesters or Fermenters of Violence?," and "Are African Americans Really Treated Worse by Law Enforcement.?" These questions have been strongly debated in American society since Black Lives Matter appeared on the scene. The future of race relations in the United States greatly depends on finding effective and peaceful answers.

The future is an open book. How Black Lives Matter and law enforcement react to current events will shape their relationship for decades to come. That is why the debate today about the role of Black Lives Matter in American society is so important.

OPPOSING
VIEWPOINTS®
SERIES

CHAPTER 1

Do Black Lives Matter, or Do All Lives Matter?

Chapter Preface

The racial divide that has plagued America in increasing intensity since the turn of the twenty-first century is evident in the arguments revolving around the very name of the organization that has spurred such heated debates. The mere mention of Black Lives Matter often prompts the same angry retort seeking to reaffirm the value of every American. That is, *all* lives matter.

The following chapter addresses both sides of the debate. Viewpoint authors that support Black Lives Matter express disbelief that anyone could misunderstand its outlook. They spotlight the point that the organization concedes equal value of every human life. Their contention is that a disproportionately larger number of recent police shootings of African Americans prove that black lives matter less than white livess in the hearts and minds of law enforcement officials. Those that agree with that assertion allude to statistics that show such inequality of treatment and back their position.

Those that maintain the opposite view offer that the high crime rate in inner cities naturally make police officers treat young African American males—in particular—with greater suspicion. Critics of Black Lives Matter contend that the higher number of confrontations with police due to the comparatively large amount of criminal activity in such areas result in more shootings and killings.

Backers of BLM cite that many of the incidents have involved unarmed blacks that were doing nothing illegal at the time. The opinions offered by many in this chapter center on the crux of the issue—that white people dealing with police under similar circumstances more often remain alive and unharmed. Black Lives Matter is simply stating a fact based on experience and data. That is, white lives matter far more than black lives matter to many in law enforcement and American society in general.

> *"One of the greatest tragedies in American history was the myth that America could flourish without blacks flourishing as persons."*

Black Lives Matter Because Black People Are Persons

Anthony B. Bradley

In the following viewpoint, Anthony B. Bradley argues that Black Lives Matter must find and articulate a moral basis for its purpose before it can be widely accepted and embraced in America. A willingness and ability to express the need for a Black Lives Matter movement will determine the success or failure of the movement. The author contends that this is because one wonders if anyone's life matters, given the waste of human life in recent years. Bradley serves as an associate professor of religious studies at King's College in New York City.

As you read, consider the following questions:

1. Does the author successfully provide a moral foundation for Black Lives Matter?
2. How has a lack of religion weakened the relationship between law enforcement and African Americans?
3. How does the author claim that the use of language widens the respect gap?

"Why Do Black Lives Matter?" by Anthony B. Bradley, Acton Institute, December 31, 2014. Reprinted by permission.

B lack lives matter." "All lives matter." These slogans may forever summarize the deep tensions in American life in 2014. Catalyzed by the deaths of Michael Brown, Eric Garner, and two New York police officers who were murdered while sitting in a police car, Americans are in the midst of a crisis of human dignity. Are we still able to articulate why anyone's life matters? We can loudly protest that "black lives matter," but it will mean nothing in the long run if we cannot explain why black lives matter.

Having desiccated our shared anthropology to the point that people are defined by the pursuit of individualistic and depersonalized rights, Americans can no longer ontologically justify the claim that anyone is worthy of dignity, love, and respect. In the current crisis, we are left to reduce some of our neighbors to depersonalized nouns: "suspect," "thug," "criminal," "felon," or "cop." This type of depersonalization is the gateway to dehumanization, because it gives us permission to suspend the requirement to treat people with dignity, even if they have broken the law.

Black lives matter because black people are persons. One of the greatest tragedies in American history was the myth that America could flourish without blacks flourishing as persons. From the founding of this country, throughout slavery, Reconstruction, the eugenics movement, and the civil rights movement, black Americans fought to establish themselves, first and foremost, as persons. At minimum we can define persons as centers of creativity, self-transcendence, communication, morality, self-direction, responsibility, choice, freedom, and spirituality, who come to know themselves in union and communion with the Triune God and other personal selves. Persons are simultaneously unrepeatable splendors with great capacity for good and also vulnerable to disordered loves that can lead to profound evil. Not only do they need moral formation; moral norms ought to shape how we structure the elements of justice in politics, jurisprudence, and the marketplace.

One of the greatest contributions that Christianity made to the world was to provide an ontological justification for human dignity and human rights. Black life matters because black people have been called to a vocation—to attain the end for which they were created in union and communion with others persons who have the same calling. Today, humans are reduced to depersonalized, abstract individuals possessing "rights" to be asserted and acquired for the purpose of self-actualization with little to no regard for the other. In a depersonalized, individualistic society people could not care less about the flourishing of their neighbors. What matters is the consumeristic flourishing of the self in a morally relativistic pursuit of desired passions. Too many Americans do not know how to distinguish between rights and passions.

In a culture that has done all it can to expunge moral virtue from the aspirations of human life, why are we surprised that we are shouting, "Black lives matter?" When human persons are not expected to be in communion with God and others, why are we surprised that the reverence due to the human person is lost? Black lives matter because persons are not autonomous, self-contained, individualistic creatures who do not need others for their flourishing. Black lives matter not simply because they are black but because blacks are persons—persons who are a necessary variable to the flourishing of others so that we all may attain the end for which we were created.

As we move into 2015, the fact remains that in order for there to be sustainable peace and justice following the events in Ferguson and New York City—that is, if we truly want to heal the wounds that divide us—we must first understand and what it means to be human. As Dr. Martin Luther King observed, "[E]very human life is a reflection of divinity, and ... every act of injustice mars and defaces the image of God in man." Advocating for black life without a moral basis is throwing sand into the wind.

| "*White people have the privilege to interact with the social and political structures of our society as individuals.*"

White People Are Complicit in Racism

John Metta

In the following viewpoint, the text of a reflection spoken to an all-white church audience, John Metta argues that only the experience of walking in the shoes of an African American person can allow a person to speak intelligently about racism. The author asserts that white people in America are largely unaffected by racism, can only view its effects from afar, and therefore cannot offer an opinion based on experience. As a man with close white and black relations, Metta indicates that blacks are more aware of the effects of intentional and unintentional segregation throughout society than whites are. Metta's writing has appeared in Medium and Al Jazeera.

As you read, consider the following questions:

1. What motivated the author to write the article?
2. According to the author, to what extent does segregation still exist in America today?
3. What point does the author make about the use of marijuana in citing how society treats its black and white citizens differently?

"I, Racist," by John Metta, Those People, April 14, 2017, https://www.thsppl.com/thsppl-articles/2017/4/14/i-racist?rq=I%2C%20Racist. Reprinted by permission.

A couple weeks ago, I was debating what I was going to talk about in this sermon. I told Pastor Kelly Ryan I had great reservations talking about the one topic that I think about every single day.

Then, a terrorist massacred nine innocent people in a church that I went to, in a city that I still think of as home. At that point, I knew that despite any misgivings, I needed to talk about race.

You see, I don't talk about race with White people.

To illustrate why, I'll tell a story:

It was probably about 15 years ago when a conversation took place between my aunt, who is White and lives in New York State, and my sister, who is Black and lives in North Carolina. This conversation can be distilled to a single sentence, said by my Black sister:

> The only difference between people in the North and people in the South is that down here, at least people are honest about being racist.

There was a lot more to that conversation, obviously, but I suggest that it can be distilled into that one sentence because it has been, by my White aunt. Over a decade later, this sentence is still what she talks about. It has become the single most important aspect of my aunt's relationship with my Black family. She is still hurt by the suggestion that people in New York, that she, a northerner, a liberal, a good person who has Black family members, is a racist.

This perfectly illustrates why I don't talk about race with White people. Even—or rather, especially—my own family.

I love my aunt. She's actually my favorite aunt, and believe me, I have a lot of awesome aunts to choose from. But the facts are actually quite in my sister's favor on this one.

New York State is one of the most segregated states in the country. Buffalo, New York, where my aunt lives, is one of the 10 most segregated school systems in the country. The racial inequality of the area she inhabits is so bad that it has been the subject of reports by the Civil Rights Action Network and the NAACP.

Those, however, are facts that my aunt does not need to know. She does not need to live with the racial segregation and oppression of her home. As a white person with upward mobility, she has continued to improve her situation. She moved out of the area I grew up in– she moved to an area with better schools. She doesn't have to experience racism, and so it is not real to her.

Nor does it dawn on her that the very fact that she moved away from an increasingly Black neighborhood to live in a White suburb might itself be an aspect of racism. She doesn't need to realize that "better schools" exclusively means "whiter schools."

I don't talk about race with White people because I have so often seen it go nowhere. When I was younger, I thought it was because all white people are racist. Recently, I've begun to understand that it's more nuanced than that.

To understand, you have to know that Black people think in terms of Black people.

We don't see a shooting of an innocent Black child in another state as something separate from us because we know viscerally that it could be our child, our parent, or us, that is shot.

The shooting of Walter Scott in North Charleston resonated with me because Walter Scott was portrayed in the media as a deadbeat and a criminal—but when you look at the facts about the actual man, he was nearly indistinguishable from my own father.

Racism affects us directly because the fact that it happened at a geographically remote location or to another Black person is only a coincidence, an accident. It could just as easily happen to us—right here, right now.

Black people think in terms of we because we live in a society where the social and political structures interact with us as Black people.

White people do not think in terms of we. White people have the privilege to interact with the social and political structures of our society as individuals. You are "you," I am "one of them." Whites are often not directly affected by racial oppression even in their own community, so what does not affect them locally has little chance of affecting them regionally or nationally. They have no need, nor often any real desire, to think in terms of a group. They are supported by the system, and so are mostly unaffected by it.

What they are affected by are attacks on their own character. To my aunt, the suggestion that "people in The North are racist" is an attack on her as a racist. She is unable to differentiate her participation within a racist system (upwardly mobile, not racially profiled, able to move to White suburbs, etc.) from an accusation that she, individually, is a racist. Without being able to make that differentiation, White people in general decide to vigorously defend their own personal non-racism, or point out that it doesn't exist because they don't see it.

The result of this is an incessantly repeating argument where a Black person says "Racism still exists. It is real," and a white person argues "You're wrong, I'm not racist at all. I don't even see any racism." My aunt's immediate response is not "that is wrong, we should do better." No, her response is self-protection: "That's not my fault, I didn't do anything. You are wrong."

Racism is not slavery. As President Obama said, it's not avoiding the use of the word Nigger. Racism is not white water fountains and the back of the bus. Martin Luther King did not end racism. Racism is a cop severing the spine of an innocent man. It is a 12 year old child being shot for playing with a toy gun in a state where it is legal to openly carry firearms.

But racism is even more subtle than that. It's more nuanced. Racism is the fact that "White" means "normal" and that anything else is different. Racism is our acceptance of an all white *Lord of the Rings* cast because of "historical accuracy," ignoring the fact that this is a world with an entirely fictionalized history.

Even when we make s*#@ up, we want it to be white.

And racism is the fact that we all accept that it is white. Benedict Cumberbatch playing Khan in *Star Trek*. Khan, who is from India.

Is there anyone Whiter than Benedict Cumberbatch? What? They needed a "less racial" cast because they already had the Black Uhura character?

That is racism. Once you let yourself see it, it's there all the time.

Black children learn this when their parents give them "The Talk." When they are sat down at the age of 5 or so and told that their best friend's father is not sick, and not in a bad mood—he just doesn't want his son playing with you. Black children grow up early to life in *The Matrix*. We're not given a choice of the red or blue pill. Most white people, like my aunt, never have to choose. The system was made for White people, so White people don't have to think about living in it.

But we can't point this out.

Living every single day with institutionalized racism and then having to argue its very existence, is tiring, and saddening, and angering. Yet if we express any emotion while talking about it, we're tone policed, told we're being angry. In fact, a key element in any racial argument in America is the Angry Black person, and racial discussions shut down when that person speaks. The Angry Black person invalidates any arguments about racism because they are "just being overly sensitive," or "too emotional," or– playing the race card. Or even worse, we're told that we are being racist (Does any intelligent person actually believe a systematically oppressed demographic has the ability to oppress those in power?)

But here is the irony, here's the thing that all the angry Black people know, and no calmly debating White people want to admit: The entire discussion of race in America centers around the protection of White feelings.

Ask any Black person and they'll tell you the same thing. The reality of thousands of innocent people raped, shot, imprisoned, and systematically disenfranchised are less important than the suggestion that a single White person might be complicit in a racist system.

This is the country we live in. Millions of Black lives are valued less than a single White person's hurt feelings.

White people and Black people are not having a discussion about race. Black people, thinking as a group, are talking about living in a racist system. White people, thinking as individuals, refuse to talk about "I, racist" and instead protect their own individual and personal goodness. In doing so, they reject the existence of racism.

But arguing about personal non-racism is missing the point.

Despite what the Charleston Massacre makes things look like, people are dying not because individuals are racist, but because individuals are helping support a racist system by wanting to protect their own non-racist self beliefs.

People are dying because we are supporting a racist system that justifies White people killing Black people.

We see this in how one Muslim killer is Islamic terror; how one Mexican thief points to the need for border security; in one innocent, unarmed Black man shot in the back by a cop, then sullied in the media as a thug and criminal.

And in the way a white racist in a state that still flies the confederate flag is seen as "troubling" and "unnerving." In the way people "can't understand why he would do such a thing."

A white person smoking pot is a "hippie" and a Black person doing it is a "criminal." It's evident in the school to prison pipeline and the fact that there are close to 20 people of color in prison for every white person.

There's a headline from the *Independent* that sums this up quite nicely: "Charleston shooting: Black and Muslim killers are 'terrorists' and 'thugs.' Why are white shooters called 'mentally ill'?"

I'm gonna read that again: "Black and Muslim killers are 'terrorists' and 'thugs.' Why are white shooters called 'mentally ill'?"

Did you catch that? It's beautifully subtle. This is an article talking specifically about the different way we treat people of color in this nation and even in this article's headline, the white people are "shooters" and the Black and Muslim people are "killers."

Even when we're talking about racism, we're using racist language to make people of color look dangerous and make White people come out as not so bad.

Just let that sink in for a minute, then ask yourself why Black people are angry when they talk about race.

The reality of America is that White people are fundamentally good, and so when a white person commits a crime, it is a sign that they, as an individual, are bad. Their actions as a person are not indicative of any broader social construct. Even the fact that America has a growing number of violent hate groups, populated mostly by white men, and that nearly *all* serial killers are white men can not shadow the fundamental truth of white male goodness. In fact, we like White serial killers so much, we make mini-series about them.

White people are good as a whole, and only act badly as individuals.

People of color, especially Black people (but boy we can talk about "The Mexicans" in this community) are seen as fundamentally bad. There might be a good one—and we are always quick to point them out to our friends, show them off as our Academy Award for "Best Non-Racist in a White Role"—but when we see a bad one, it's just proof that the rest are, as a rule, bad.

This, all of this, expectation, treatment, thought, the underlying social system that puts White in the position of Normal and good, and Black in the position of "other" and "bad," all of this, is racism.

And White people, every single one of you, are complicit in this racism because you benefit directly from it.

This is why I don't like the story of the good samaritan. Everyone likes to think of themselves as the person who sees someone beaten and bloodied and helps him out.

That's too easy.

If I could re-write that story, I'd rewrite it from the perspective of Black America. What if the person wasn't beaten and bloody? What if it wasn't so obvious? What if they were just systematically challenged in a thousand small ways that actually made it easier for you to succeed in life?

Would you be so quick to help then? Or would you, like most White people, stay silent and let it happen?

Here's what I want to say to you: Racism is so deeply embedded in this country not because of the racist right-wing radicals who practice it openly, it exists because of the silence and hurt feelings of liberal America.

That's what I want to say, but really, I can't. I can't say that because I've spent my life not talking about race to White people. In a big way, it's my fault. Racism exists because I, as a Black person, don't challenge you to look at it.

Racism exists because I, not you, am silent.

But I'm caught in the perfect Catch 22, because when I start pointing out racism, I become the Angry Black Person, and the discussion shuts down again. So I'm stuck.

All the Black voices in the world speaking about racism all the time do not move White people to think about it– but one White John Stewart talking about Charleston has a whole lot of White people talking about it. That's the world we live in. Black people can't change it while White people are silent and deaf to our words.

White people are in a position of power in this country because of racism. The question is: Are they brave enough to use that power to speak against the system that gave it to them?

So I'm asking you to help me. Notice this. Speak up. Don't let it slide. Don't stand watching in silence. Help build a world where it never gets to the point where the Samaritan has to see someone bloodied and broken.

As for me, I will no longer be silent.

I'm going to try to speak kindly, and softly, but that's gonna be hard. Because it's getting harder and harder for me to think about the protection of White people's feelings when White people don't seem to care at all about the loss of so many Black lives.

> "For white adults, support for Black
> Lives Matter is divided among
> party lines, with just 4% of white
> Republicans expressing support for
> the movement, in comparison to 29%
> of white Democrats."

Black Lives Matter Is Confusing to Voters

Hannah Spencer

In the following viewpoint, Hannah Spencer examines the representation of the Black Lives Matter vs. All Lives Matter debate during the controversial 2016 presidential campaign. The differences in opinion on the subject expressed by Republican Donald Trump, Democrat Hillary Clinton, and other fringe candidates, were sharply divided and gave voters clear partisan distinctions regarding their opinions on race relations in America. Trump clearly sided with the "all lives matter" viewpoint while Clinton stressed that everyone should listen to and understand the messages those in the Black Lives Matter movement were expressing. Spencer was a British exchange student at the University of Texas at Austin and an intern at Vote Smart when she wrote this viewpoint.

"Black Lives Matter and/or All Lives Matter?" Vote Smart, November 14, 2016. Reprinted by permission.

As you read, consider the following questions:

1. What did fringe presidential candidates Gary Johnson and Jill Stein state about Black Lives Matter?
2. What did Pew Research reveal about the clarity of the message put out by Black Lives Matter?
3. What incident brought Black Lives Matter national attention?

BlackLivesMatter and/or #AllLivesMatter? Both hashtags (trending topics on social media) have ignited a national conversation on the use of police brutality, and the mistreatment of minorities in America. While they don't have to exist separately, the way they have been discussed in the political arena of the 2016 election has pitched them against each other. One such culmination of this was in the Democratic Presidential Debate, when candidates were asked "Do black lives matter or do all lives matter?"

Despite existing since 2012, the #BlackLivesMatter movement didn't receive significant media attention until the months after the Ferguson protests in relation to the killing of Michael Brown. In the 4 hours following the not-guilty verdict, the hashtag was used 92,784 times. #BlackLivesMatter is self-described as "a call to action and a response to the virulent anti-Black racism that permeates American society." The intention of the #BlackLivesMatter hashtag is to broaden the conversation around state violence to include all of the ways in which Black people are intentionally left powerless at the hands of the state.

In public discussion surrounding the movement, #AllLivesMatter has been used as an alternative statement. Unlike the Black Lives Matter movement, it has no specific origin, but instead developed throughout debate as being a less-exclusionary statement. South Carolina's First Black Senator since Reconstruction, Tim Scott, used the statement in an interview on CNN, citing that this statement allows us to see what we have in common and bridges racial divides. The All Lives Matter movement therefore places inclusion as a motivator behind it's use of the phrase.

However, publicly using one statement over the other can be seen as controversial, as seen in the phrasing in the question in the Democratic Debate. Those who use "All Lives Matter" are accused of denouncing the events that only Black individuals specifically experience, whereas those using "Black Lives Matter" are accused of being exclusionary to other discriminated groups.

How Did the Presidential Candidates Use the Phrase/s?

Presidential Nominee for the Republican Party, Donald Trump, has been vocal about his support for the phrase "All Lives Matter". He argues that "the fact is all lives matter - that includes Black and it includes White and it includes everybody else." He also weighed in on the Black Lives Matter movement itself, saying "I think they're trouble. I think they're looking for trouble . . . I was watching the head of Black Lives Matter being interviewed the other night. And I said to myself, give me a break. All lives matter."

Democrat Presidential Nominee Hillary Clinton, on the other hand, stated that "we do need to listen to those who say Black Lives Matter. Too many black Americans, especially young men, feel like their lives are disposable."

Similarly, The Green Party's Jill Stein has pledged her support for the Black Lives Matter Movement. In her statement on Bernie Sander's decision to "work with Hillary Clinton," she cites his support for Black Lives matter as being an important contribution to the rising demand for change among average Americans.

Gary Johnson, nominee of The Libertarian Party, was questioned on his position regarding Black Lives Matter, after an audience member during debate suggested that Libertarians respect, but do not embrace the Black Lives Matter movement. Johnson responded "Yes, Well I do. And I'll come back to the drug war. If you're of color, there's a four times more likelihood that

Obama Explains BLM

Many politicians have taken up the rallying cry of "all lives matter" to criticize the Black Lives Matter movement for focusing on specific injustices done to African Americans. During a criminal justice panel discussion with Police Chief Charlie Beck of the LAPD and Editor-in-Chief Bill Keller of the Marshall Project on Thursday afternoon, President Barack Obama took on that claim and explained why "black lives matter" is an important statement.

"I think the reason that the organizers used the phrase "black lives matter" was not because they were suggesting nobody else's lives matter," he said. "What they were suggesting was, there is a specific problem that is happening in the African American community that's not happening in other communities. And that is a legitimate issue that we've got to address."

But the meaning of the phrase has been perverted by media pundits and some members of law enforcement, who argue that it is inflammatory rhetoric. The phrases "all lives matter" and "blue lives matter" sprang up in direct response to activists who have mobilized against police brutality and attacks on black lives.

"It started being lifted up as 'these folks are opposed to police, and they're opposed to cops, and all lives matter.' So the notion was somehow saying black lives matter was reverse racism, or suggesting other people's lives didn't matter or police officers' lives didn't matter," he said.

Obama then pointed out that saying "black lives matter" is not about reducing the importance of other groups.

"I think everybody understands all lives matter. Everybody wants strong, effective law enforcement. Everybody wants their kids to be safe when they're walking to school. Nobody wants to see police officers, who are doing their jobs fairly, hurt," he continued.

Today, black lives matter is not just a rallying cry. Due to activists' efforts to elevate the conversation about police brutality against black communities, the conversation has become a main talking point in the 2015–2016 election cycle. During the first Democratic debate, candidates were asked, "do black lives matter or do all lives matter?"

"Obama Explains The Problem With 'All Lives Matter,'" by Carimah Townes, ThinkProgress, October 22, 2015.

you'll end up behind bars than if you're not of color. And I think so much of 'shoot first' has to do - has its roots in the drug war."

President Barack Obama has aimed to provide clarity on the debate. He argues that the reason the organizers use the phrase "Black Lives Matter" is because there is a specific problem that is happening in the African American community that's not happening in other communities. He continued, "this isn't a matter of us comparing the value of lives. This is recognizing that there is a particular burden that is being placed on a group of our fellow citizens."

Despite this, the public still remains confused and conflicted on the debate. A study conducted by Pew Research found that only 12% of whites and 33% of blacks say they understand the goals of Black Lives Matter. In particular, for white adults, support for Black Lives Matter is divided among party lines, with just 4% of white Republicans expressing support for the movement, in comparison to 29% of white Democrats.

This issue is still hotly debated among the public and politicians alike. Moreover, public debate is likely to continue about what #AllLivesMatter means as a response to the #BlackLivesMatter movement. If these two social movements continue to be exclusive from each other, then the stances candidates take on them may change future legislation to come.

> "*Black Lives Matter activists participate in the preferential option for the oppressed by recognizing the unjust suffering of a specific group of people in a particular time and place, lamenting the injustice, and working for change. And whether they intend to or not, those who say, 'All Lives Matter' shut down the conversation.*"

Of Course All Lives Matter— That's Not the Point

Mike Jordan Laskey

In the following viewpoint Mike Jordan Laskey combines his religious background, which most often is tied to conservatism in the United States, with a sense of justice and unfairness in American society to provide an understanding of the motivation of Black Lives Matter. Laskey expresses that understanding in positively comparing the movement to those who embrace the "all lives matter" credo that he sees as empty and argumentative. He argues that the mere statement "all lives matter" is an attempt to shut down any discussion about the viability of Black Lives Matter. Laskey is director of Life and Justice Ministries in the diocese of Camden, New Jersey.

"Saying 'All Lives Matter' Misses the Mark," by Mike Jordan Laskey, The National Catholic Reporter Publishing Company, August 11, 2016. Reprinted by permission.

As you read, consider the following questions:

1. What almost-daily occurrence gave the author inspiration to write this article?
2. How does the author tied Black Lives Matter in with the tenets of Christianity throughout the piece?
3. What Biblical passage does the author relate to the Black Lives Matter vs. All Lives Matter debate?

A lmost every day, I drive past an auto repair shop that has a huge banner covering its street-facing side. It reads, "All Lives Matter / God Bless & Protect Our Police Officers."

On the surface, there's nothing about these two sentences I disagree with at all: I believe that each and every person matters because all are created in the image and likeness of God, and that it is good to pray for the protection of police officers in the line of duty. But each time I pass the banner, I catch myself feeling angry and sad.

The phrase "All Lives Matter" has appeared over the past few years as a direct retort to the Black Lives Matter movement, which itself was launched in response to the repeated killings of unarmed black men, women and children by law enforcement around the country. The movement is laser-focused on this injustice and our collective inability to address it in any meaningful way.

This systemic killing and abuse of power is wrong, the movement asserts, and in the face of this unimaginable injustice, it is essential to proclaim that black lives matter.

"All lives matter," some reply, most often in defense of police officers, who are also the targets of violence. So what's wrong with the wider scope of this phrase?

A few weeks ago, I saw a viral comic strip by Kris Straub floating around the internet. It reminded me of the way God acts in the Moses and the burning bush story and helped me realize why "All Lives Matter" is so off the mark.

In the beginning of the Book of Exodus, the Israelites are Pharaoh's slaves in Egypt. Moses, shepherding a flock of sheep, comes to Mount Horeb one evening, and God appears to him in the burning bush. "I have observed the misery of my people who are in Egypt; I have heard their cry on account of their taskmasters," God says (3:7). "Indeed, I know their sufferings, and I have come down to deliver them from the Egyptians, and to bring them up out of that land to a good and broad land, a land flowing with milk and honey. …" God tells Moses he will send him to Pharaoh to demand liberation for the Israelites.

Sometimes, the teaching that God loves everyone equally can lead us to turn God into some sort of divine Switzerland—neutral in every conflict. But it is because God loves everyone equally that he stands up with and for those who are targeted by injustice. God hears the cry of the oppressed and then gets involved. He will "come down" to "bring them up," in the words of the passage. God has a special love for those who are hurting, and so he gets involved on their behalf. In other words, he turns his attention first to the house that's on fire—which is just what the Black Lives Matter movement is trying to do.

This belief about the nature of God's love inspires a Catholic principle called the preferential option for the poor and vulnerable, which is all about how we prioritize. (The "poor and vulnerable" part of the principle doesn't fit perfectly in a discussion about Black Lives Matter; maybe a more suitable phrasing for what the movement is practicing would be "preferential option for the oppressed.") We don't evaluate how healthy our society is by how well those at the top are doing, but by how those at the bottom are faring. The preferential option calls us to imitate God's special love for the victims of injustice as we're setting up our social structures.

Black Lives Matter activists participate in the preferential option for the oppressed by recognizing the unjust suffering of a specific group of people in a particular time and place, lamenting the injustice, and working for change. And whether they intend to or not, those who say "All Lives Matter" shut down the conversation.

They're changing the subject. The phrase could very well be, "No, you're wrong. All lives matter." It fails to acknowledge the reality of the suffering caused by the killing of black men, women, and children by law enforcement.

Further, "All Lives Matter" misses the point because it suggests that saying that black lives matter is the same as saying that only black lives matter. The movement is intentionally narrow, shining a spotlight on one horrific injustice. Of course every person matters, and of course there are so many other injustices that require attention, including violence directed toward police officers. But as Black Lives Matter activist DeRay McKesson said in a recent interview with CNN, you don't go to a breast cancer rally and shout, "Colon cancer matters!"

This strategy reminds me of Jesus's ministry in the Gospels. He also approached injustice with a tight focus, confronting individual injustices one at a time, depending on his context. Blogger Stephen Mattson noted this similarity in a 2015 post: "Instead of saying all lives matter, Jesus said, 'Samaritan lives matter,'" Mattson writes. "Instead of saying all lives matter, Jesus said, "Women's lives matter." Through a series of specific, personal encounters and actions, Jesus built his case that every person is important. But he took on the injustices one at a time.

So, if our aim is to act like Jesus, then it is a good thing to pay attention and respond to individual injustices as we learn about them—to lend our support to urgent causes like Black Lives Matter and to resist glib responses like "All lives matter" that effectively paper over the problem. Because as long as there are any specific individuals or communities who feel like their lives don't matter, our work to protect the God-given dignity of every person will be incomplete.

> *"As to the question of whether Black*
> *Lives Matter holds some form of*
> *racial bias because they care about*
> *black lives, I give a firm 'no.' Even*
> *if some black activists do hold bias*
> *against white people, fighting for the*
> *rights and welfare of black people is*
> *not in and of itself racist."*

We Must Respond to White Ignorance

Mary Joyce

In the following viewpoint, Mary Joyce responds to critics of Black Lives Matter and its agenda point by point. The author tackles all issues and arguments offered by those that disagree with the BLM agenda and tactics, particularly those that fall into the category of what she terms "white nonsense." Included are claims that Black Lives Matter perpetrates violence, that black-on-black crime causes far more needless deaths than police brutality, and that not all cops are racist. Joyce acknowledges the truth to all the above, but asserts that such facts do not eliminate the need to address the spate of killings perpetrated by law enforcement against black citizens. Joyce writes for Meta-Activism, an organization that strives to create social change.

"Sensible Responses to White Nonsense," by Mary Joyce, August 14, 2015. Reprinted by permission.

As you read, consider the following questions:

1. How does the author respond to those that claim Black Lives Matter is hurting its own cause?
2. Why did the author allude to a rally held by Democratic presidential candidate Bernie Sanders to make a point?
3. What argument was given to justify Black Lives Matter priority to police shootings over gang killings in inner cities?

I recently decided to start responding to white critics of Black Lives Matter.

Black activists are busy. They have a revolution to run and do not have time to be dealing with white nonsense. But I do. Below are some common critiques of Black Lives Matter, along with appropriate responses.

Remember, white allies, it's better to call in than call out. Calling in makes instances of white ignorance and insensitivity teaching moments, instead of f--- -you moments. While f--- -you may feel good, calling white people in to being decent and empathic human beings is to everyone's advantage.

BLM activists, if I get anything wrong, please let me know.

Critique 1: But the Violence! (ie, misplaced outrage)

White Nonsense: Is violence ever acceptable? Looting innocent business owners, firing shots at police, etc. in Ferguson. Carving the name of the cop who shot Brown on the skin of a pig, roasting it and then eating it's head in front of the Ferguson Police Dept? Angry and rude is far from this level of violence that is being carried out.*

Reasoned Response: Which violence are we choosing to talk about? The cause for these protests is the shooting of unarmed black people, yet that is not the violence that seems to be most upsetting to you. Why do you think that is, [Meredith]?

White Nonsense: I am in no way in defense of the abuse of police power or the mistreatment of innocent blacks. But to fight violence with violence is not the answer. Innocent people are suffering from these protests. This is inexcusable and to make excuses for it is dangerous.*

Reasoned Response: [Brad] I know that the anger of oppressed people can be disconcerting and upsetting, whether it's symbolic acts, words, or destruction of property. They are angry at the institutions that protect us and do not protect them and they are angry at us for supporting these institutions. The question is, which violence offends us more: the smashing of a police car or the murder of a black child? If the answer is the former, which it is for a lot of white people, then that needs to change. We need to shift our empathy and identification from the institutions of oppression to those who are oppressed.

Critique 2: Annoyance at Hearing About Oppression

White Nonsense: I think [race is] a bit of a potential third rail in American politics. Unfortunately, I think a lot of white voters get tired of hearing about it.*

Reasoned Response: [Tom], white voters get tired of hearing about racism? That is no doubt true, just as men get tired of hearing about sexism or the rich get tired of hearing about the struggles of the poor or non-veterans gets tired of hearing about PTSD. I certainly hope that's not true of you. That's also not the country I want to live in. Hearing about the pain of others is a cause for compassion, not annoyance.

Critique 3: You're Hurting Your Cause! (ie, concern trolling)

White Nonsense: Those interruptions do nothing to stop people dying in the streets, they only give the movement a bad name.*

White Nonsense: Disruptions like this do a big disservice to a great cause. Anything you'll say in these minutes will be overshadowed by the fact that you hijacked the microphone.*

Reasoned Response: Well, let's look at the evidence, [Kelsey]. If we're talking about [the interruption of Bernie Sanders' speech] then we can see that in the week following that action:

- August 8th (evening): Sanders names a black activist, Symone Sanders, as Press Secretary. Her first official action is to introduce him at another event in Seattle.
- August 9th: After an event in Portland, Sanders went out of his way to meet with Black Lives Matter activists.
- August 10th: Sanders' campaign adds a new set of racial justice policies to his campaign platform,including action on physical violence against black people, disenfranchisement, and economic exclusion. The platform won praise from Deray McKesson who has emerged as a media spokesperson for BLM.
- August 11th: Black Lives Matter activists get invited onto the stage. They open Sanders' event in Los Angeles.

So I'd say that disruptive tactic did help their cause. Remember that black lives > white feelings. If you are arguing the reverse, ask yourself why.

Critique 4: But Black-on-Black Violence!

White Nonsense: But what about all the other young black murder victims? Nationally, nearly half of all murder victims are black. And the overwhelming majority of those black people are killed by other black people. Where is the march for them? (source)

Reasoned Response: Regardless of harm members of a group do to each other, harms being done to that group by others still need to be addressed. In the wise words of Cornel West (whom I once saw walking through an airport!), "we have to distinguish between state-sponsored violence and violence against black people owing to actions black people do to each other. Both are important, but they're not the same thing."

Diverting attention away from police using this argument is a classic derailment and lets abusive police officers off the hook. Police officers with hair-trigger tempers who have no respect for the law are a danger to everyone, so diverting attention away from their bad acts harms all citizens.

Critique 5: #BlackLivesMatter Is Itself Racist

White Nonsense: What about the argument that the Black Lives Matter movement is Racist in itself by only concerning themselves with black victims of police violence?*

Reasoned Response: There are a variety of ways of defining the word racism. Some argue that "racism equals power." According to this interpretation, black and other people of color can be biased or prejudiced, but they can't be racist. This is because, according to this interpretation, racism = bias based on skin color + control over institutions that can do harm as a result of those biases. So a black person can be biased, but they cannot be racist because they lack control over institutions to do harm to white people as a result of that bias.

However… this is not the most common definition. The prevailing definition focuses exclusively on bias or individual treatment as a result of bias. The Merriam-Webster Dictionary, for example, defines Racism as both "poor treatment of or violence against people because of their race," which anyone could do, and "the belief that some races of people are better than others," which could also apply to a person of any skin color.

Fortunately for logical argument, it is not necessary to resolve this definitional question to respond to the above criticism of Black Lives Matter. As to the question of whether Black Lives Matter holds some form of racial bias because they care about black lives, I give a firm "no." Even if some black activists do hold bias against white people (which, to be honest, I find quite understandable), fighting for the rights and welfare of black people is not in and of itself racist.

To show specific support for one group is not inherently oppositional to other groups. For example, if I am fighting for access to HIV treatment I am not inherently expressing bias towards people who are HIV-negative. If I am fighting for housing for homeless youth I am not inherently biased against adults with homes. If I am fighting for animal welfare I am not inherently anti-human.

The causes we care about are tied to our experiences, our identities, and who we love. Each of us must fight for the causes that move our hearts. This isn't bias. This is the engine of human rights and human progress.

Critique 6: Racism Doesn't Exist Because White People Suffer Too

White Nonsense: Being white doesn't protect you from this class system, making it a blame game is absolutely racist. Being white doesn't make you automatically rich, doesn't protect your home, won't promise you a job or a life. It certainly won't protect you from homelessness or poverty.

Reasoned Response: Identity is intersectional. This means that while some elements of our identity privilege us, others disadvantage us. For example, I am privileged by my whiteness, my middle class background, and being cisgendered, but I am also disadvantaged by being queer and being female.

To take your example, a person who is able-bodied has greater privilege than one who is not. To accurately articulate that whiteness is being used to divide and disadvantage people who do not have this trait is not racist. Ignoring this abuse is.

Black people are disadvantaged in our society, so are mentally ill people, so are poor people, so are transgender people…. We live in a very unequal society.

Critique 7: Not All Cops…

White Nonsense First Responder: Any advice on the "not all cops are bad" bull----?

Reasoned Response: Like "not all white people" and "not all men," this line of criticism really doesn't stand up to logic. Can you imagine if the Catholic Church had given this response to the pedophile priest scandal? What if the Vatican spokesperson had said, "Yes, some of our priests are pedophiles, but not all of them are. In fact, most of our priest are not pedophiles. For that reason, we see no need to act. In fact, we don't even understand what you are all so worried about." People would have been legitimately outraged.

If there is an abusive element in any institution of public trust or power, it needs to be dealt with. Saying there are only a few abusers (whether this is true or not) does not change this fact.

* denotes direct quote from a white person

> "*The Justice Department cited numerous cases of 'tactically unsound and unnecessary actions' among officers, including shooting unarmed suspects; shooting at vehicles without justification; using a taser on an unarmed, naked 65-year-old mentally ill woman; and purposely depositing gang members in rival territory.*"

Police Are Abusing the African American Community

Judith Valente

In the following viewpoint, Judith Valente provides an account of the scathing report from the Department of Justice after an investigation of the Chicago police department. Chicago has received much negative attention for suffering through the worst gang warfare and the most black youth homicides in the country. But the report states that rather than playing a significant role in reducing tensions, Chicago law enforcement has exacerbated the problem through its unfair and sometimes brutal treatment of black and Hispanic citizens. The author argues that documentation such as the DOJ report should make clear to any doubters that black lives are valued as lesser. Valente is a journalist, poet and essayist.

As you read, consider the following questions:

1. What were the most serious charges made against Chicago police in the Department of Justice report?
2. How many homicides were reported in Chicago in 2016?
3. How was it suggested in this article that religious leaders can help ease tensions in the inner city of Chicago?

For the second time in little over a year, Chicago residents have received a blistering report detailing widespread instances of police abuse, aimed particularly at African American and Hispanic communities.

City officials reacted to the latest report from the U.S. Department of Justice by promising to change policies and procedures, expand training and mentoring and equip all officers with body cameras by the end of this year. But many community activists are asking a central question: How do you change hearts and minds?

"You can change the training at the academy and retrain all of the current officers, but the biggest issue is changing the culture," said Rev. Michael Pfleger, a longtime activist whose parish, St. Sabina, is in an economically struggling neighborhood on Chicago's South Side. "You can change all the rules and still have prejudice and hate."

The Justice Department report was initiated after several high profile police shootings of citizens, including the death of Laquan McDonald, an African American teenager shot 16 times by a white officer. The officer subsequently was charged with murder, and the incident sparked widespread protests after it was revealed law enforcement had tried to conceal an official police video of the shooting.

The Justice Department cited numerous cases of "tactically unsound and unnecessary actions" among officers, including shooting unarmed suspects; shooting at vehicles without justification; using a taser on an unarmed, naked 65-year-old mentally ill woman; and purposely depositing gang members in rival territory.

Federal investigators said some Chicago department practices also put officers at unnecessary risk. "We found that officers exhibit poor discipline when discharging their weapons and engage in tactics that endanger themselves and public safety, including failing to await back-up when they safely could and should; using unsound tactics in approaching vehicles; and using their own vehicles in a manner that is dangerous."

City officials repeated many of the same promises that followed the release of a similar report last year, ordered by Mayor Rahm Emanuel. The mayor said all officers will be equipped with body cameras by the end of 2017. Chicago police superintendent Eddie Johnson has called for revising use of force procedures and expanding training and mentoring of officers. But many community activists say something deeper is necessary—the repair of trust.

"The first thing I thought of when I read the report was the victims. Behind the statistics of the report are all the lives that have been impacted," said Jedidiah Brown, a leader of the local Black Lives Matter movement.

Mr. Brown said officers need to be seen more "among the people," outside of crime calls. "You have to be honest and acknowledge the frustration and hurt," he said.

That is likely to be a difficult and lengthy process. In a statement, the Chicago police union complained that the Justice report had been "rushed." Comments on a blog popular with the rank and file police suggested that the new administration of President Donald J. Trump might be more sympathetic to the police point of view. These types of investigations usually result in local law enforcement entering into consent decrees that lay out widespread changes. The new administration in Washington could slow or even ignore that process.

For many in the city, change cannot come too quickly. In 2016, Chicago experienced its most violent year in two decades, with 762 homicides—more than in the larger cities of New York and

Los Angeles combined. The violence is largely confined to a few economically disadvantaged neighborhoods on the city's South and West Sides. Officials attribute the surge in shootings in part to the splintering of the city's powerful street gangs, at least partly driven by the teardown of Chicago's infamous public housing projects in recent years. Large, centrally directed groups have broken down into less-disciplined factions that might operate within a few blocks of each other or on a single corner.

Many activists say the increased scrutiny of law enforcement has caused officers to back off on policing in the most volatile neighborhoods, adding to the crisis.

Mr. Brown and others also acknowledge the role residents must play in making their neighborhoods safer. "Public safety rests on the shoulders of the residents. The problem is, they have been so disempowered," Mr. Brown said. He called for the police to cooperate with residents in "organizing channels of information-sharing and building community."

Father Pfleger said Chicago may need to invite outside experts to oversee a dialogue between police and minority residents aimed at restoring trust. "The question we need to ask isn't how do we tolerate each other, but how do we respect each other," Father Pfleger said.

He called on Catholic priests in the city to address race relations more explicitly from the pulpit and to initiate conversations on race and violence at the parish level. "This issue by and large has not been addressed in the Catholic parishes, the Protestant churches, the synagogues and mosques. Why do we continue to run from this issue? Why aren't we breaking down walls and holding these conversations? We can't expect government to do it," Father Pfleger said.

Dr. Jerry Hiller, a psychologist who leads a popular series of lunchtime talks on faith in daily life called "Repair My House" at St. Peter's in the Loop parish, says the city also needs to address the emotional and psychological factors underlying Chicago's social problems.

Across the United States, "what is breaking down is a sense of commonality," Dr. Hiller said. "There is uncontrollable anger, a feeling of powerlessness, self-contempt, of not belonging and isolation," he added.

Still, Dr. Hiller says he has seen firsthand concrete change come to troubled neighborhoods. Several years ago, he said residents in his former far North Side neighborhood of Rogers Park banded together to rid the area of increasing gang activity. They formed crime watches and agreed to call police and cooperate when they had information on a crime. They went to court to drive out slum landlords and demanded the city do something about junk cars left on the street and trash in public parks.

"When people feel they belong and have a place in the community, they cooperate," Dr. Hiller said.

Outgoing Attorney General Loretta Lynch traveled to Chicago earlier in January to personally present the Justice Department findings. She also sounded a note of hope. Speaking recently of the legacy of Dr. Martin Luther King Jr., she said in words that could easily apply to Chicago: "If it does come to pass that we do enter a period of darkness, let us remember—that is when dreams are best made."

Chicago has witnessed its period of darkness. It is now time for the city's many factions to work on realizing the dream of a safer, more caring city.

Periodical and Internet Sources Bibliography

The following articles have been selected to supplement the diverse views presented in this chapter.

Hilary Hurd Anyaso "Northwestern poll: Most African-Americans view Black Lives Matter as an effective movement," Northwestern Now, October 19, 2017. https://news.northwestern.edu/

Perry Bacon, Jr. "Black Lives Matter has shifted national debate, despite controversial reputation," NBC News, July 12, 2016. https://www.nbcnews.com/news/nbcblk/black-lives-matter-has-shifted-national-debate-despite-controversial-reputation-n607526

Jesse Damiani "Every time you say 'all lives matter' you are being an accidental racist," Huffington Post, July 16, 2017. https://www.huffingtonpost.com/jesse-damiani/every-time-you-say-all-li_1_b_11004780.html

Ryan Gabrielson. Eric Sagara and Ryann Grochowski Jones "Deadly force, in black and white," ProPublica, October 10, 2014. https://www.propublica.org/article/deadly-force-in-black-and-white

Juliana Menasce Horowitz and Gretchen Livingston "How Americans View the Black Lives Matter Movement," Pew Research Center, July 8, 2016. http://www.pewresearch.org/fact-tank/2016/07/08/how-americans-view-the-black-lives-matter-movement/

Ian Olasov "How did 'all lives matter' come to oppose Black Lives Matter? A philosopher of language weighs in," Slate.com, July 18, 2016. http://www.slate.com/blogs/lexicon_valley/2016/07/18/all_lives_matter_versus_black_lives_matter_how_does_the_philosophy_of_language.html

Curry Petersen-Smith "Black Lives Matter: A new movement takes shape," International Socialist Review, Issue 96. https://isreview.org/issue/96/black-lives-matter

Tim Philbin "Is Black Lives Matter vs. all lives matter the only choice?" Study Break, July 13, 2016. https://studybreaks.com/2016/07/13/is-black-lives-matter-vs-all-lives-matter-the-only-choice/

Does Black Lives Matter Have the Wrong Focus?

Chapter Preface

The sheer numbers give verbal ammunition to critics of Black Lives Matter. How can the organization focus on occasional, albeit tragic and highly publicized, killings of African Americans by police when thousands of gang-related murders destroy so many black lives in inner cities across the United States every year? they argue. Should BLM not be focusing its attention and efforts into curbing black-on-black crime that too often results in homicides rather than the comparatively small number of incidents with law enforcement that conclude in the death of one individual?

The following chapter places a spotlight on that question and attempts to express the views of those that either believe BLM sets its sights in the wrong direction or that its focus is justified. Among the contentions in favor of Black Lives Matter included in the viewpoints in this chapter is that it indeed has sought to intervene against gang violence that has taken the lives of many young blacks, but such efforts have gone unrecognized by the media because they do not attract strong television ratings or newspaper and Internet readership. The organization and its backers cite various efforts to improve lives in Black America that are unrelated to police shootings. Such efforts that go largely unreported are touched upon here as a defense of Black Lives Matter.

Many believe that criticism of BLM removes the spotlight from where it belongs—on the police. It is argued here that their inability to develop a trusting and friendly relationship with those in black communities have fostered an adversarial mindset on both sides. Critics of Black Lives Matter do not disagree that police officers have struggled to build trust. They blame gangs and high crime rates rather than the men and women in blue. And they fault BLM for not doing more to solve that problem.

> "*The Black Lives Matter movement acknowledges the crime problem, but it refuses to locate that crime problem as a problem of black pathology. Black people are not inherently more violent or more prone to crime than other groups.*"

Myths About Black Lives Matter Should Be Debunked

Leroy Barber

In the following viewpoint Leroy Barber tackles individually each of what he considers myths about Black Lives Matter. Included is the focus of this chapter—that Black Lives Matter concerns itself solely with police brutality against young African Americans while ignoring inner-city gang violence that has resulted in far more black lives lost. Among the others is that Black Lives Matter is anti-white and anti-police, both of which Barber contends is untrue. Rather, he asserts, the Black Lives Matter movement seeks to change systemic racism and policies that inherently target African Americans. Barber is a pastor, writer, and activist.

As you read, consider the following questions:

1. How does the author use scripture as a basis for his arguments?
2. What does the author claim as a counter to the contention that the only issue Black Lives Matter cares about is police brutality against African Americans?
3. What issues targeted by Black Lives Matter does the author believe are more important than getting black voters to the polls?

You are worthy to take the scroll and
to open its seals, because you were
slain, and with your blood you
purchased for God persons from
every tribe and language and people
and nation. You have made them
to be a kingdom and priests to serve
our God, and they will reign on
the earth.

—Revelation 5:9-10

My heart dropped as I watched the face of Michael Brown's mother and listened to her screams as she looked upon her son lying in the street, not being allowed to approach his body. His dead body lay there for four hours and his mom, family, and friends looked on with horror. The scene was played over and over and the more it played, the more it seemed as though the life of this young man meant nothing. Many had that same thought and #BlackLivesMatter captured it. The scene of Michael Brown's death, along with many others, was the catalyst to the creation of #BlackLivesMatter. The statement was needed to remind us that we did indeed matter, even if only to ourselves. We are declaring it for ourselves, for our children, and for generations to come.

The Black Lives Matter movement is currently causing controversy and debate, even within the church. InterVarsity Christian Fellowship weathered quite a bit of criticism when #BlackLivesMatter was highlighted at the Urbana 15 Student Missions Conference. Some Christians wonder how we can embrace a movement that seems in certain ways to uphold values that are contrary to Christian ideals. Why should the church, some ask, care about BLM when its agenda seems to be suspicious and even dangerous? But perhaps we need to look at the emergence of BLM in another way: as a part of God's plan to bring us into relationship with one another across race and cultural barriers.

Revelation 5 pictures all of God's people together worshiping the Lamb who was slain on our behalf. On that day we will together make up a kingdom of priests, and that kingdom will be composed of people from every language, ethnicity, culture, and nationality. The barriers that divide us will be gone, though the skin colors and speech that distinguish us will remain. Indeed, the very diversity that now causes us so much trouble will then be a notable part of the glory and wonder of our combined worship.

To be sure, the picture in Revelation 5 is of a future time. But that future reality is far truer than our present tumultuous attempts to just get along. The reality is that our lives are bound together in God's kingdom and that we can together begin to experience his ultimate plans even now.

The text says that they will reign on the earth. The location of this glorious future reality is right here, where we're living now. Can we imagine for a moment what this will look like—our barrios and neighborhoods being places of uninterrupted shalom, our slums and "projects" lush and beautiful centers of human flourishing, our war-torn cities and countrysides gardens of peace and joy?

It seems pretty clear that we have not yet experienced all that God has for us as a redeemed and reconciled community of believers. It is time we started reaching across the barriers that continue to separate us.

Debunking the Myths of #BlackLivesMatter

The Black Lives Matter movement was born out of the continued struggle of black people in the United States and around the world. It's a call for blacks to be respected as human beings. This movement has given voice to many who are being oppressed and denied rights that should be given to all people. I have felt this violation of basic human rights profoundly as I've watched men and women killed in the streets by police—with many of these participating officers not even having to answer in court. Black Lives Matter seems to have sparked a resurgence of the civil rights movement and features a younger generation who is taking ownership. Although the movement understands the history of civil rights and the role of the church, it has decided to do some things differently. This has come under major scrutiny from many. There has been a great deal of misunderstanding about #BLM, and I would like to debunk some of the myths and misunderstandings that surround it.

Myth number 1: The movement doesn't care about black-on-black crime.

The idea that black-on-black crime is not a significant political conversation among black people is patently false. In Chicago, long maligned for its high rates of intraracial murder, members of the community have created the Violence Interrupters to disrupt violent altercations before they escalate. Those who still insist on talking about black-on-black crime frequently fail to acknowledge that most crime is intraracial. 93 percent of black murder victims are killed by other black people. 84 percent of white murder victims are killed by other white people. The continued focus on black-on-black crime is a diversionary tactic whose goal is to suggest that black people don't have the right to be outraged about police violence in vulnerable black communities just because those communities have a crime problem. The Black Lives Matter movement acknowledges the crime problem, but it refuses to locate that crime problem as a problem of black pathology. Black people are not inherently more violent or more prone to crime than other groups. But black people are disproportionately poorer, more likely to be targeted by police and arrested, and more likely to attend poor or failing schools. All of these social indicators place a black person at greater risk for being either a victim or a perpetrator of violent crime. To reduce violent crime, we must fight to change systems rather than demonizing people.

Myth number 2: It's a leaderless movement.

The Black Lives Matter movement is a leader-full movement. Many Americans of all races are enamored with Martin Luther King Jr. as a symbol of leadership and of what real movements look like. But the Movement for Black Lives (another name for the BLM movement) recognizes many flaws with this model. First, focusing on heterosexual, cisgender black men frequently causes us not to see the significant amount of labor and thought leadership that black women provide to movements, not only in caretaking and auxiliary roles, but on the front lines of protests and in the strategy sessions that happen behind closed doors Moreover, those old models of leadership favored the old over the young, attempted to silence gay and lesbian leadership, and did not recognize the leadership possibilities of transgender people at all. A movement with a singular leader or few visible leaders is vulnerable, because those leaders can be easily identified, harassed, and killed, as was the case with Dr. King. But by having a leader-full movement, BLM addresses many of these concerns. BLM is composed of many local leaders and many local organizations including Black Youth Project 100, the Dream Defenders, the Organization for Black Struggle, Hands Up United, Millennial Activists United, and the Black Lives Matter national network. We demonstrate through this model that the movement is bigger than any one person. And there is room for the talents, expertise, and work ethic of anyone who is committed to freedom.

Myth number 3: The movement has no agenda.
Many believe the Black Lives Matter movement has no agenda—
other than yelling and protesting and disrupting the lives of white
people. This is also false. Since the earliest days of the movement in
Ferguson, groups like the Organization for Black Struggle, the Black
Lives Matter network, and others have made a clear and public
list of demands. Those demands include swift and transparent
legal investigation of all police shootings of black people, official
governmental tracking of the number of citizens killed by police
(disaggregated by race), the demilitarization of local police forces,
and community accountability mechanisms for rogue police
officers. Some proposals like the recently launched Campaign
Zero by a group of Ferguson activists call for body cameras on
every police officer. But other groups are more reticent about this
solution, since it would lead to increased surveillance and possible
invasions of privacy, not to mention a massive governmental
database of information about communities of color that are
already heavily under surveillance by government forces.

Myth number 4: It's a one-issue movement.
Although it is true that much of the protesting to date has been
centered on the issue of police brutality, there's a range of issues
that the movement will likely push in years to come. One is the
issue of our failing public education system, which is a virtual
school-to- prison pipeline for many black youth. Another is the
complete dismantling of the prison industrial complex. Many of
the movement's organizers identify as abolitionists, which in the
twenty-first-century context refers to people who want to abolish
prisons and end the problem of mass incarceration of black and
Latino people. Three other significant issues are problems with safe
and affordable housing, issues with food security, and reproductive-
justice challenges affecting poor women of color and all people
needing access to reproductive care. As I frequently like to tell
people, this movement in its current iteration is still very new.
Things take time to mold and take shape. Give it some time to find

its footing and its take on all the aforementioned issues. But the conversations are on the table largely because many of the folks doing work on the ground came to this movement through their organizing work around other issues.

Myth number 5: The movement has no respect for elders.
The BLM movement is an intergenerational movement. If you ever have occasion to attend a protest action, you will see black people of all ages, from the very young to the very old, standing in solidarity with the work being done. Certainly there have been schisms and battles between younger and older movers about tactics and strategies. There has also been criticism from prior civil rights participants. BLM has a clear rejection of the respectability politics ethos of the civil rights era, namely a belief in the idea that proper dress and speech will guard blacks against harassment by the police. This is a significant point of tension within black communities, because in a system that makes one feel powerless to change it, belief in the idea that a good job, being well-behaved, and having proper dress and comportment will protect you from the evils of racism makes it feel like there's something you can do to protect yourself, that there's something you can do to have a bit of control over your destiny. This movement patently rejects such thinking in the face of the massive evidence of police mistreatment of black people across all classes and backgrounds. All people should be treated with dignity and respect, regardless of how one looks or speaks.

Myth number 6: The black church has no role to play.
Many know that the black church was central to the civil rights movement, since many black male preachers became prominent civil rights leaders. This current movement has a very different relationship to the church than in movements past. Black churches and black preachers in Ferguson have been on the ground helping since the early days after Michael Brown's death. But protesters patently reject any conservative theology that focuses on keeping the peace, praying copiously, or turning the other cheek. Such

calls are viewed as a return to passive respectability politics. But local preachers and pastors like Rev. Traci Blackmon, Rev. Starsky Wilson, and Rev. Osagyefo Sekou have emerged as what I call "Movement Pastors." With their radical theologies of inclusion and investment in preaching a revolutionary Jesus (a focus on the parts of Scripture where Jesus challenges the Roman power structure) and their willingness to think of church beyond the bounds of a physical structure or traditional worship, they are reimagining what notions of faith and church look like and radically transforming the idea of what the twenty-first-century black church should be.

Myth number 7: The movement hates white people.
The statement "black lives matter" is not an anti-white proposition. Contained within the statement is an unspoken but implied "too," as in "black lives matter, too," which suggests that the statement is one of inclusion rather than exclusion. However, those white people who continue to mischaracterize the affirmation as being anti-white are suggesting that in order for white lives to matter, black lives cannot. That is a foundational premise of white supremacy. It is antithetical to what the Black Lives Matter movement stands for, which is the simple proposition that black lives also matter. The Black Lives Matter movement demands that the country affirm the value of black life in practical and pragmatic ways, including addressing an increasing racial wealth gap, fixing public schools that are failing, combating issues of housing inequality and gentrification that continue to push people of color out of communities where they have lived in for generations, and dismantling the prison industrial complex. None of this is about hatred for white life. It is about acknowledging that the system already treats white lives as if they have more value, as if they are more worthy of protection, safety, education, and a good quality of life than black lives are. This must change.

Myth number 8: The movement hates police officers.
Police officers are people. Their lives have inherent value. This movement is not an anti-people movement; therefore, it is not an

anti-police-officer movement. Most police officers are just everyday people who want to do their jobs, make a living for their families, and come home safely at the end of their shift. This does not mean, however, that police are not implicated in a system that criminalizes black people, that demands that they view black people as unsafe and dangerous, that trains them to be more aggressive and less accommodating with black citizens, and that does not stress that we are taxpayers who deserve to be protected and served just like everyone else. Thus the Black Lives Matter movement is not trying to make the world more unsafe for police officers; it hopes to make police officers less of a threat to communities of color. We reject the idea that asking officers questions about why one is being stopped or arrested, about what one is being charged with, constitutes either disrespect or resistance. We reject the use of military-grade weapons as appropriate policing mechanisms for any American community. We reject the faulty idea that disrespect is a crime, that black people should be nice or civil when they are being hassled or arrested on trumped-up charges. And we question the idea that police officers should be given the benefit of the doubt when it comes to policing black communities. Increasingly, the presence of police makes black people feel less rather than more safe. And that has everything to do with the antagonistic and power-laden ways in which police interact with citizens generally and black citizens in particular. Police officers must rebuild trust with the communities they police. Not the other way around.

**Myth number 9: The movement's
primary goal should be the vote.**
Recently the Democratic National Committee endorsed the Black Lives Matter movement. The BLM network swiftly rejected that endorsement. While voting certainly matters, particularly in local municipalities like Ferguson, movement members are clear that voting for policies and politicians whose ultimate goal is to maintain a rotten and unjust system is counterproductive. The movement cares about national politics, and many participants

have sought to make presidential candidates responsive to their political concerns. But there is deep skepticism about whether the American system is salvageable, since it's so deeply rooted in ideas of racial caste. In this regard, the BLM movement, together with the Occupy movement of years past, is causing a resurgence of a viable, visible, and vocal (black) left in national politics. Moving some issues of import onto the 2016 election agenda should therefore be viewed as a tactic, not a goal. The goal is freedom and safety for all black lives. And that goal is much bigger than one election.

Myth number 10: There's not actually a movement at all.
Until Bernie Sanders sought the attention of Black Lives Matter participants, many were unwilling to acknowledge that a new racial justice movement even existed. For the record, since August 2014, there have been more than 1,030 protest actions held in the name of Black Lives Matter. We should take notice of this new generation of freedom fighters as they make their mark in history. A new generation of protest music has come forth, with songs from Janelle Monae, Prince, J. Cole, Lauryn Hill, and Rick Ross. The first national convening in July drew over one thousand participants. There is a new consciousness and a new spirit seeking justice, and the participants carrying the torch show no signs of slowing down.

I'm aware that there are challenges for some Christians when it comes to Black Lives Matter. I am not saying (and neither do I believe they are saying) that you have to agree with everything. Giving support to BLM doesn't mean you agree with everything—there are differing opinions even within the movement itself. What we should agree on is that this movement has helped bring voice to the frustrations and feelings of many black people who have felt neglected, looked past, and ignored as human beings. The need to feel seen as a person is real.

I am not requesting that you agree with everything you have read about Black Lives Matter. I am advocating for a listening ear, healthy dialogue, and love. This is where loving hard people—

including our enemies—begins to take shape in our hearts. Can you love and disagree? Can you love and honor another's humanity in spite of the differences?

For Those Who Are Not Black

I recently talked to a white, male, middle-aged friend and leader in the nonprofit world, and he confessed that there is no one black in his inner circles, and for that matter, not a single person of color. This was a lament, and in it he was truly confessing and wanting to repent. He wanted to start again.

The big question then was how. How does a white man in his fifties make new friends? It's hard for anyone to look outside their social circles for new friends, and it's is especially hard for middle-aged folks like him and me.

This is one of the more insidious things about racism in America. We don't fully know how to engage outside our own circles. This has caused injustice to burn out of control and racism to run rampant, paralyzing us when it comes to practical ways to find reconciliation.

But There Are Ways to Start.
Here's a List of Suggestions:

- Read books written by blacks and discuss them.
- Shop in a mall or store on the other side of town routinely.
- Watch different TV shows.
- Listen to a different radio station.
- Go to a different coffee shop.
- Go see movies with mostly black casts.
- Attend a black church routinely (once a month or quarter).
- Give to an organization led by a person of color.
- Go see a play written and performed by black writers and actors.
- Visit the African American museum close to you.

- Go to a sporting event with a black coworker at your place of employment.
- Take your church small group to a protest or rally.
- Set up regular prayer time or attend a prayer meeting at a black church.
- Put your kids in an activity where they will interact with black children.

Please don't get me wrong. We have some very deep racial problems and injustice to work through, and these things are by no means the answer. But they may at least move us a step closer in understanding by creating space for new friendships to emerge.

Taking the Time

I've thought about why certain people seem to be able to embrace those who are different, whereas others struggle with getting along. It seems to me that the most important factor is patience—that the people who succeed at getting past differences and misunderstandings are those willing to take the time to get to know other people.

Those who embrace others don't let stereotypes or even their own experiences predetermine the possibilities for new relationships. They risk getting to know someone even when it might be dangerous. They disregard the misplaced counsel of their close friends who think the idea of engaging others who are different is impossible or foolish. They ignore the racist taunts and name-calling that might come along with taking risks for relationships and for having the ideal that perhaps we can get to a new place. They accept that the world may misunderstand them. They remain anchored to the certain knowledge that God will bless their obedience and will reveal a bit more of himself in the other person they are called to love.

Embracing the call to relationships means . . .

- taking time to get to know one another.
- taking time to trust one another.

- taking time to see things in a new way.
- seeking to enjoy another person's ways when they differ from our own.
- wanting what is right even if that means being alone and misunderstood.
- being true and honest about who our friends are even when they are from the other side of the tracks.
- loving deeply even when we don't always understand.
- praying for the person who hurts us.
- giving to something we don't fully understand because friendship is more important.
- going against our own culture for the sake of a friend.
- celebrating with strangers.
- being vulnerable in a strange place.
- listening to one another's stories even when don't understand.
- even being willing to die for those you consider your enemy.

All of these things enable us to start loving people we once hated. They allow us to start going to places we would never have gone before. We risk going into unfamiliar places in pursuit of true community. But once we achieve true community, we find we have new places where we are known, loved, and appreciated, where we accept advice from unlikely sources and where improbable people take risks for our sakes.

It's all good, it's all sweet, it's all risky, and it's all somehow possible.

The promise of Revelation 5 only eludes us because we aren't willing to go the distance with people who are different from us. I believe with all my heart that our joy in loving community is incomplete if that community is monocultural. We can only know God's full blessing when we are loving all of our neighbors, when we have put Christ's kingdom first, ahead of our prejudices, our comfort, and our culture's ways. We can and must love the Samaritans, the Babylonians, and the Ninevites in our lives.

What a testimony that would be for the world around us! The mark of the follower of Christ is love for one another. But the world is not impressed by those who love only their own family, their own tribe or fraternity. It's when we allow the love of Christ in us to be expressed through us to those of other ethnicities and nationalities that the unbelieving culture will sit up and take notice.

This is why the case of love and forgiveness by the Charleston families moves us so much. When we see the forgiveness of Jacob DeShazer toward his Japanese captors, we recognize the supernatural in it. We know that the compassion of African American slave women for the children of their masters is not a purely human thing, but that Christ's love animates it. When we understand that the relatives of Jim Elliot and Nate Saint gave the rest of their lives to bring God's love to the tribal people who killed them, we stand in awe in the presence of the Prince of Peace.

I've had glimpses in my own life of the supernatural joy of loving those who are vastly different from me. I've seen many who have taken chances and come out on the other side with incredible relationships that last a lifetime. My life has been made so much fuller by loving different people from around the world and across the street.

Why don't you give it a shot? Why don't you grab an opportunity to go to a place where you're not supposed to be? Why don't you invest your time and treasures in a relationship? Why don't you become foolish in the world's eyes to see if the impossible can come to life? We are all one people, and we have more in common than we think. We just don't push ourselves to embrace those commonalities. Our culture and forces all around us tell us not to trust, not to reach across those walls, not to listen to one another's stories, not to consider the other side of the story, not to believe God's picture of his kingdom on earth. What if God meant for us to find our true selves only in relationship with one another? What if all we have to do is take a step toward those relationships— and then God will manifest the power that raised Christ from the dead?

I know the road before us is not going to be easy. I expect it to be filled with hard places and difficult people. The work involved may seem overwhelming as we press for unity, peace, and equality. But we know what the end could look like— what God has shown us in

Revelation 5. This doesn't mean moving past the hard relationships too quickly, or discounting the need for the difficult confrontation of systems of power and injustice. In fact, we need to enter into this with eyes wide open, fully aware of the trials inherent to such a commitment to relationship.

We are in the middle of a very divisive moment. The winds of discord are blowing hard. We are in a conflict-ridden conversation and it's troublesome. But our current way of living and relating will only lead to destruction. There is hope, and that hope rests in our ability to honor one another in the strength of deep relationship. We'll use one of the most powerful Forces we know to weave us into harmony, and allow the essence of our cultures, creativity, and hearts to help us solve our largest problems. We are God's creation, made from one place. We are different because God is so vast, alike because he is one. Let's embrace the Spirit of God that rests in us all.

> "*Activism advocating that black lives matter could have much more moral authority, and could be taken much more seriously, if it focused on actions devaluing black lives. These have very little to do with white cops and everything to do with self-destructive black behavior.*"

Gang Violence Is BLM's Own Worst Enemy

Derryck Green

In the following viewpoint Derryck Green argues that Black Lives Matter should focus on widespread black-on-black crime instead of police mistreatment of African Americans. But one cannot easily claim racism in the author's opinion. Green, after all, is African American and a member of the of the national advisory council of the Project 21 black leadership network. He contends that creating efforts that change the behavior of black youth in inner city communities would not only lift those communities and the people that live there, but also force outsiders to embrace Black Lives Matter complaints about racism in American law enforcement. Green received an M.A. in Theological Studies from Fuller Theological Seminary and is currently pursuing his doctorate in ministry at Azusa Pacific University.

"The 'Black Lives Matter' Slogan Ignores Self-Destructive Behavior," by Derryck Green, National Center for Public Policy Research. Reprinted by permission.

As you read, consider the following questions:

1. What steps does the author believe Black Lives Matter should take to create more positivity to its cause?
2. Statistics from 1980 to 2008 show that blacks are how many times more likely to be victims of homicide than whites?
3. What divisive issue often debated by the religious right does the author cite as evidence that black lives do not matter enough to African Americans?

B lack Lives Matter" is a great slogan. As a black man, I agree that black lives matter just as much as the lives of any of our racial counterparts.

But chanting, marching and hashtag activism isn't going to work unless we also are willing to see the big-picture problems affecting black America.

Here's a hint: making black lives matter has little to do with institutional racism, white privilege and white cops.

One website organizing people pushing "black lives matter" calls it "a slogan under which black people can unite to end state sanctioned violence both in Ferguson, but also across the United States of America… to end the insidious and widespread assault on black life." It states "Black people make up a mere 13 percent of the U.S. population [but] make up more than a third of those killed in officer-involved shootings across the country."

Perhaps. But the virtuous goal of promoting the perceived value of black lives in the manner now demanded by radical community activists is tragically misguided.

Activism advocating that black lives matter could have much more moral authority, and could be taken much more seriously, if it focused on actions devaluing black lives. These have very little to do with white cops and everything to do with self-destructive black behavior.

There is a disparity regarding violent death in the black community. We are killing our own at an alarming rate. According to a U.S. Department of Justice analysis, most murders are intraracial and "93 percent of black victims were killed by blacks" between 1980 and 2008. Yet Attorney General Holder, President Obama and Reverend Sharpton haven't wanted a national conversation about this shocking figure.

In a black-white comparison, black homicide victimization rates were around six times higher than for whites. Furthermore:

- Blacks were 47.4 percent of all homicide victims and 52.5 percent of offenders.
- Blacks accounted for 62.1 percent of all drug-related homicide victims compared to 36.9 percent for whites. Over 65.6 percent—almost two-thirds—of all drug-related homicide offenders were black as compared to 33.2 percent being white.
- Blacks were 44.1 percent of felony murder victims and almost 59.9 percent of the offenders.

It's not like things improved under Obama's leadership. According to FBI statistics for 2012, 2,412 of 2,648 cases of black homicide had a black perpetrator.

This, to me, qualifies as an "insidious and widespread assault on black life." Yet those claiming black lives matter fixate on Michael Brown and Eric Garner while virtually ignoring the thousands of black-on-black murder victims who remain largely nameless and faceless except to their loved ones.

The internecine war doesn't begin there. It actually begins in the womb. As deadly as black-on-black crime can be, the most dangerous place for a black child is still in the womb.

While blacks make up only around 13 percent of the American population, the Centers for Disease Control and Prevention reported black abortions accounted for nearly 35.7 percent of all abortions performed in 2010. In Mississippi, blacks accounted

What About Black-on-Black Crime?

Black Lives Matter has done the nation a service by forcing Americans to reckon with a horrifying spate of police killings of unarmed African Americans. Without the movement, the names Eric Garner and Walter Scott wouldn't resonate. Nor would Sandra Bland, who died in police custody and whose name was invoked during the most recent presidential debate. Despite this, Black Lives Matter has been severely taken to task, if not outright scorned, for its focus on police killings when, as its critics readily note, people in black neighborhoods are often at much more danger of being killed by other black people.

Why, they ask, hasn't the Black Lives Matter movement been more concerned with—in wording sometimes fraught with condescension—"black-on-black crime?"

It's a criticism typically associated with the political right, frequently thought (and frankly, frequently meant) to suggest that what black people need is to simply comport themselves differently, rather than endlessly complain about the depredations of (presumably) white police. However, even without such acrid, tribalistic intent, it's possible to think BLM's mission is currently incomplete.

I have consistently decried excessive stop-and-frisk policies and loudly supported the protests in Ferguson, Mo.—even as I recognize that the facts surrounding Michael Brown's death were not what many initially supposed—and those in New York responding to Garner's killing. Clearly, the tensions between cops and black Americans are keeping America from getting past race. I am regularly assailed from the right for these views.

And yet I maintain that Black Lives Matter should develop a second wing, devoted to rooting out the minority of criminals in black neighborhoods who kill with such abandon that in almost any big city in America, reading of such events over a weekend is so typical it barely makes news.

In response, some have asked a valid question: What do people like me suggest the movement does in this vein, given that there have been efforts to stanch—yes, I'll use the phrase—black-on-black crime for decades? Even today, Stop the Violence marches are a regular feature in black communities. How much good, then, would it do for BLM to join the legions of people simply calling for an end to violence, to so little effect? None, probably.

"Black Lives Matter Should Also Take on 'Black-on-Black Crime,'" by John McWhorter, The Washington Post, October 22, 2015.

for 71.7 percent of all abortions, despite blacks comprising only around 37 percent of the population.

Similarly, a report from the New York City Department of Health and Mental Hygiene found more black babies were killed by abortion (31,328) in New York City than were born (24,758) in 2012—totaling 42.4 percent of all abortions performed there.

Black lives matter? Not only is it questionable if black lives really do matter to blacks themselves, but one could also sincerely question if deep self-hate is responsible for motivating blacks to kill themselves off with the recklessness that seems to permeate our actions.

Combining the black victims of abortion and black-on-black homicides, we are facing an assault on black lives that has nothing to do with racist, white cops.

If we don't take our own lives seriously, why should we expect or demand that anyone else do so?

I believe black lives matter. It's more than an Internet hashtag to me. But black lives should matter to black folk at least as much as they matter to others. Black lives have to matter just as much when blacks take them.

> "How can the national spotlight
> on police brutality be used as an
> opportunity to make broader changes
> that answer the fundamental
> question posed by Black Lives
> Matter: What does it look like to
> value black life?"

Black Lives Matter Should Expand Its Focus

Garrett Felber

In the following viewpoint, Garrett Felber argues that police reform is only one issue in the larger struggle for black freedom. Through an examination of police violence against people of color throughout modern African American history and the community's fight for other rights, the author contends that the Black Lives Matter movement should capitalize on the recent attention brought to police brutality against people of color and expand its advocacy for a host of other, equally important issues to the African American community.

Felber is assistant professor of history at the University of Mississippi and a scholar of twentieth-century African American history and social movements.

"What Black Lives Matter Means Beyond Policing Reform," by Garrett Felber, The Conversation, July 11, 2016. https://theconversation.com/what-black-lives-matter-means-beyond-policing-reform-62332. Licensed under CC BY 4.0 International..

As you read, consider the following questions:

1. What does Alton Sterling's murder highlight, according to the author?
2. Over what issue did the Emergency Committee for Unity on Economic and Social Problems subcommittee on law enforcement threaten to disband?
3. What event in 1965 led to greater funding for militarized police departments according to the viewpoint?

A fter the killing of five police officers in Dallas last week by a lone gunman, where does the Black Lives Matter movement go?

Black Lives Matter co-founder Alicia Garza answered this question, saying she anticipated that the Dallas shooting would "create the conditions for increased security, surveillance and monitoring of protesters ... an expansion of the police state, rather than reduction of one."

As Garza points out, the failure of the dash cam and body cameras to document what happened in the killing of Alton Sterling in Louisiana highlights the limitations of technology as the centerpiece of reform. It had even been the focal point of Al Sharpton's 2014 National March Against Police Violence.

As Garza argued, "There has to be something bigger than that."

As a scholar of 20th-century African American history and social movements, I have focused my research on community activism in the 1950s and 1960s against police brutality in major cities such as Los Angeles and New York. Police violence often opened a space for organizing people of color from across the religious and political spectrum around core issues facing their communities. But these coalitions were often tenuous. And the idea of police reform being the most important issue within the larger black freedom struggle has always been contentious.

The challenge facing us now is twofold. First, how can we think about addressing the problem of racialized police violence beyond professional and mechanical reforms?

And second, how can the national spotlight on police brutality be used as an opportunity to make broader changes that answer the fundamental question posed by Black Lives Matter: What does it look like to value black life?

The Challenge of Black Unity

This tension was at play more than a half-century ago in a brief coalition formed in Harlem called the Emergency Committee for Unity on Economic and Social Problems. The organization was founded in the summer of 1961 by civil rights and labor organizer A. Philip Randolph.

The group was originally formed to protest housing discrimination and the rise of unpoliced drug use in Harlem. The committee represented a wide swath of the Harlem activist community, including national civil rights figures like Bayard Rustin and black nationalists such as Lewis Michaux, "Pork Chop" Davis and Malcolm X.

The Emergency Committee for Unity on Economic and Social Problems was built on the premise of black unity around three action programs: unemployment, housing, and law and order enforcement. The *Pittsburgh Courier* immediately hailed it as a "beacon of light for other communities."

But just months after its founding in August 1961, the subcommittee on law enforcement resolved to disband if the Emergency Committee for Unity on Economic and Social Problems would not focus on the issue of police brutality. Among the subcommittee's recommendations were a civilian review board that would include representation from the community, a greater representation of African Americans and Puerto Ricans within the police department and intensive human relations training on race within the police department.

By the following year, these and other political divisions led to a fracturing of the committee. Randolph turned his focus to organizing the 1963 March on Washington for Jobs and Freedom at which Martin Luther King Jr. delivered his "I Have a Dream" speech. However, the march only loosely touched upon calls for police reform and marginalized both women and black nationalists from its program. Instead, it focused on ending school segregation and job discrimination, establishing a nationwide minimum wage and public job training, and enforcing the 14th Amendment to protect the voting rights of southern blacks.

Meanwhile, Malcolm X had moved to Los Angeles following a case of police violence which left one Muslim man dead and another paralyzed after an attack on the Nation of Islam's mosque. No officers were indicted, and 14 men were charged with assault and resisting arrest, nine of whom were eventually convicted.

Police Reform

Los Angeles was rife with discrimination and accounts of police brutality in communities of color. In 1962, the NAACP published a 12-page report documenting 10 major cases of brutality in the city. Roy Wilkins had even compared the police in Los Angeles "next to those in Birmingham, Alabama."

Yet, the Los Angeles Police Department maintained a national reputation as one of the modern exemplars of policing during the 1950s. Meanwhile, the ACLU and NAACP had been fighting for police reform in Los Angeles for over a decade, including repeated calls for a civilian review board.

In part, Police Chief William Parker's vision for a modernized police department appeared to reflect those called for by community activists, then and now. This included human relations training and a more diverse police force serving in these communities.

But Parker's understanding of "diversity" was that everyone could be a "minority group member… any of which can be, and often has been discriminated against." Training bulletins even illustrated this concept to police officers by showing them how it would feel to be called by derogatory phrases such as "fuzz" and "cop."

Professionalization meant training police officers to eradicate racist ideas through practice. As Parker proudly told a police chief conference in 1955:

> Intolerance has become a victim of enforced order – habit has won out over belief.

Modernization meant using empirical data to justify racist outcomes. The heavy use of police in communities of color, he explained, was simply "statistical – it is a fact that certain racial groups, at the present time, commit a disproportionate share of the total crime."

Beyond Police Reform

Policing in Los Angeles became even more emblematic of the modern police state after the violent arrest of a young black man led to the Watts uprising in 1965. The sheriff's department demonstrated the use of helicopters during the rebellion, and in turn earned the largest Office of Law Enforcement Assistance grant ever (US$200,000) for an air surveillance program. As historian Elizabeth Hinton writes, "A new era in American law enforcement had begun."

Today, the left-leaning Bernie Sanders has called for police to "demilitarize" from this buildup of tanks, riot gear and advanced weaponry which began after Watts. Yet, his suggestion to make police departments look like the communities they serve also mirrors Parker's language of professionalization and modernization from 50 years ago. Calls for citizen review boards, still seen as radical by many police departments, are simply attempts at accountability and lawfulness for those charged with enforcing the law.

The relationship between police reform and other broader black freedom struggles that were so pronounced in the Emergency Committee for Unity on Economic and Social Problems and the March on Washington continue today. The March on Washington's call for a national minimum wage in 1963 is still a central point of contention for the Democratic Party in our current presidential primary. The Voting Rights Act, which was one of the chief victories of the civil rights movement, has been significantly rolled back.

So how can Black Lives Matter take us beyond basic questions of police reform?

Attorney Johnnie Cochran, famous for his role as defense attorney for O.J. Simpson, worked as an assistant on the 1963 trial in Los Angeles involving the Nation of Islam. He later recalled that although such cases were difficult to win, "the issue of police abuse really galvanized the minority community. It taught me that these cases could really get attention."

The issue at stake, then, is how to take this opening and not only begin to secure justice for the lives lost to police violence, but also to expand on questions about what it means to value black life. This can be done, I believe, by continuing to center trans and queer people of color, by remaining unapologetically black and by joining in solidarity with labor struggles.

In the aftermath of Dallas, when the media will recycle old tropes to make "Black Power" synonymous with violence, Black Lives Matter must continue to think bigger and broader. As Michelle Alexander pointed out several days ago, this is not about fixing police, this is about fixing our democracy.

> "*One of the most well-demonstrated types of implicit bias is the unconscious association between black individuals and crime. That association can influence an officer's behavior, even if he or she doesn't hold or express explicitly racist beliefs.*"

Psychology Can Improve Cop-Community Relations

Kirsten Weir

In the following viewpoint Kirsten Weir applies the wide-ranging area of psychology to the Black Lives Matter Movement and argues that the mindsets and worldviews of police officers have resulted in a spate of shootings of unarmed black males. One contention is that rampant violent crime in the inner cities give law enforcement officials a different psychological reality when potential confrontations arise with young black males. One suggestion expressed here is psychological training intended to reduce bias and prejudice, as well as more community policing that creates greater interaction with black citizens and builds trust. Weir is a science writer whose work has been published in APA's Monitor on Psychology, Current Health, and The Scientist.

"Policing in Black & White," by Kirsten Weir, Monitor on Psychology, December 2016, Vol. 47, No. 11, p.36. Copyright © 2016 American Psychological Association. Reproduced with permission. No further reproduction or distribution is permitted without written permission from the American Psychological Association.

As you read, consider the following questions:

1. What state was cited in the article as requiring classes in racial bias for its police officers?
2. How might a police chase of a black perpetrator affect a potentially biased officer psychologically?
3. What statistics are cited in this article that indicate that white officers are more likely to use force against a black person than a white person under the same circumstances?

D o you believe police are implicitly biased against black people?" When NBC newsman Lester Holt asked Hillary Clinton this question in the first presidential debate, it was a sure sign the science of implicit bias had jumped from the psychology journals into the public consciousness—and that racial bias in law enforcement has entered the national dialogue.

There's evidence of racial disparities at many levels of law enforcement, from traffic stops to drug-related arrests to use of force. But the roots of those disparities aren't always clear. Experts point to systemic problems as well as the implicit (largely unconscious) biases mentioned in the debate. To be sure, those biases aren't unique to police. But in matters of criminal justice, implicit bias can have life-altering implications.

Social media has turned a spotlight on cases of racial discrimination. As the list of black citizens killed by nonblack officers grows, tensions between black communities and police are running high. "It's a nuanced problem but people continue to take a polarized view," says Jack Glaser, PhD, a social psychologist at the University of California, Berkeley. "It's not productive to demonize police."

Glaser says police departments are eager for solutions that will reduce racial disparities. "Police chiefs know what the stakes are," he says. Policymakers, too, are keen to take action. In October, for instance, the New Jersey attorney general issued a directive requiring mandatory classes in racial bias for police officers in the state. Psychologists, meanwhile, have the skills to understand discrimination and point to evidence-based solutions. "This is an area that's worth a lot of investment in research, and important for psychologists to think about," Glaser says.

Evidence of Inequality

With more than 15,000 law enforcement agencies across the country operating at the federal, state and local levels, there is no "typical" police department. Still, evidence for racial disparities is growing. Most of those data focus on the treatment of black civilians by white officers. In an analysis of national police-shootings data from 2011–14, for example, Cody T. Ross, a doctoral student in anthropology at the University of California, Davis, concluded there is "evidence of a significant bias in the killing of unarmed black Americans relative to unarmed white Americans." The probability of being black, unarmed and shot by police is about 3.5 times the probability of being white, unarmed and shot by police, he found (PLOS One, 2015).

Other studies conflict with that finding. Harvard University economist Roland G. Fryer Jr., PhD, examined more than 1,000 shootings in 10 major police departments and found no racial differences in officer-involved shootings. Fryer did, however, find that black civilians are more likely to experience other types of force, including being handcuffed without arrest, pepper-sprayed or pushed to the ground by an officer (National Bureau of Economic Research, 2016).

Those disparities don't seem to arise from the fact that black Americans are more likely to commit crimes. Supporting this point is research by Phillip Atiba Goff, PhD, a social psychologist at the University of California, Los Angeles, co-founder of the Center for Policing Equity. Goff, Glaser and colleagues reviewed data from 12 police departments and found that black residents were more often subjected to police force than white residents, even after adjusting for whether the person had been arrested for violent crimes (Center for Policing Equity, 2016).

Other data show that black people are also more likely to be stopped by police. Stanford University social psychologist Jennifer Eberhardt, PhD, and colleagues analyzed data from the police department in Oakland, California, and found that while black residents make up 28 percent of the Oakland population, they accounted for 60 percent of police stops. What's more, black men were four times more likely than white men to be searched during a traffic stop, even though officers were no more likely to recover contraband when searching black suspects (Stanford SPARQ, 2016).

And in Falcon Heights, Minnesota, where cafeteria worker Philando Castile was fatally shot by a nonblack officer in July after being pulled over for a broken taillight, statistics released by the local St. Anthony Police Department showed that about 7 percent of residents in the area are black, but they account for 47 percent of arrests.

The Police Officer's Dilemma

Many factors can account for the differences in treatment at the hands of police. In some jurisdictions, explicit prejudice still occurs, says John Dovidio, PhD, a social psychologist at Yale University who studies both implicit and explicit prejudice. Many police departments and officers take a paramilitary approach to law and order, and sometimes adopt an "us-versus- them" attitude toward black communities, he says. "There can be a lot of dehumanization that occurs in the conversations people have, and that's explicit."

In many cases, however, the biases come from unconscious or unintentional beliefs. "A large proportion of white Americans have these [implicit] biases, and it's hard to expect police officers to be any different," Dovidio says.

Implicit biases are attitudes or stereotypes that can influence our beliefs, actions and decisions, even though we're not consciously aware of them and don't express those beliefs verbally to ourselves or others. One of the most well-demonstrated types of implicit bias is the unconscious association between black individuals and crime. That association can influence an officer's behavior, even if he or she doesn't hold or express explicitly racist beliefs.

Goff describes implicit bias as a kind of identity trap. "They're situations that trap us into behaving in ways that are not consistent with our values," he says.

Joshua Correll, PhD, a psychologist at the University of Colorado, has explored one facet of implicit racial bias in a series of laboratory studies since 2000. He developed and tested a paradigm known as "the police officer's dilemma," using a first-person-shooter video game. Participants are presented with images of young men, white and black, holding either guns or innocuous objects such as cellphones or soda cans. The goal is to shoot armed targets but not unarmed targets.

The researchers found that participants shoot armed targets more often and more quickly if they're black rather than white, and refrain from shooting more often when the target is white. The most common mistakes are shooting an unarmed black target and failing to shoot an armed white target (*Journal of Personality and Social Psychology*, 2002).

But experiments with police officers show a more complex pattern. Similar to community participants, officers showed evidence of bias in their reaction times, more quickly reacting to armed black targets and unarmed white targets—in other words, targets that aligned with racial stereotypes. But those biases evident in their reaction times did not translate to their ultimate decision to shoot or not shoot (*Journal of Personality and Social Psychology*, 2007). Still, that's only part of the story. In later work, Correll found special unit officers who regularly interact with minority gang members were more likely to exhibit racial bias in their decision to shoot. When officers' training and experiences confirm racial stereotypes, those biases appear to hold more sway over their behavior (*Personality and Social Psychology Bulletin*, 2013).

Bad Habits

While research points to some patterns in implicit bias, we still have a lot to learn about the ways that biases influence people's decisions and behavior in the real world, says David M. Corey, PhD, a police psychologist and founding president of the American Board of Police and Public Safety Psychology. "Yes, implicit bias can affect us. The more important questions are, which persons are affected, and under what conditions?"

Yet while those questions remain unanswered, many police departments and policymakers have skipped ahead to a different one: What can be done to reduce implicit bias? "The police officers I've worked with are looking for effective ways to reduce implicit or unintended bias, and they welcome advice based on psychological evidence, not politics," says Corey.

Under pressure from the public, many police departments have implemented implicit bias workshops and trainings. That could be premature, says Corey. "We feel like we have to do something, but sometimes the action we take proves to be merely window dressing," he says. "My worry is that could cause a police agency to think they're doing enough, or that the monies being spent will prohibit spending for other areas, including research."

That hasn't stopped some departments from moving forward, however—a step that concerns Glaser and others who think evidence should come before implementation. "There are contractors that provide [implicit bias training], but there's zero evidence that what they do has an impact," Glaser says. "We don't know how to lastingly change implicit biases, particularly those as robust and prevalent as race and crime—and not for lack of trying."

Recently, psychologist Calvin K. Lai, PhD, at Harvard University, and colleagues tested nine different interventions designed to reduce implicit racial biases. Some interventions aimed to introduce participants to exemplary individuals that ran counter to traditional stereotypes, for example. Other strategies included priming participants to consider multicultural attitudes, or teaching participants strategies to create implementation intentions (such as repeating to themselves, "If I see a black face, I will respond by thinking 'good.'"). In two studies with more than 6,300 participants, all of the interventions reduced implicit prejudice in the short term. But none of those changes lasted more than a couple of days following the intervention—and in some cases, the effects vanished within a few hours (*Journal of Experimental Psychology*, 2016). "Implicit associations are habits of mind," Dovidio says. "And habits are really hard to change."

That's not to say there's no value in training officers. But rather than trying to eliminate their unintentional biases, it might be more fruitful to stack the deck so that officers are less likely to act on those biases. "Character is a weak predictor of behavior, but situations are strong predictors of behaviors," Goff says. And changing situations can be more feasible than changing ingrained stereotypes.

Imagine, for example, officers chasing a perpetrator after a crime has occurred. "As they chase the person, it's building up their adrenaline. All of the biases they have come together like a perfect storm," Dovidio says—a storm that can lead to excessive force. To circumvent that possibility, he says, some police departments have implemented a policy that the officer who chases a suspect should not be the one to initiate subsequent steps, such as booking the suspect or leading the interrogation. "You try to build in structures and procedures that help overcome the tendencies," he explains.

Creating protocols and checklists for various law-enforcement situations can also help remove bias from the equation, adds Tom Tyler, PhD, a professor of law and psychology at Yale Law School. Federal authorities, for example, use such checklists when deciding whether to search airline travelers for drugs: Did the person use an alias? Did they pay for their tickets with cash? Are they using evasive movements? So far, checklists haven't been rolled out for everyday street stops, Tyler says, though such protocols could help reduce bias when officers decide whether to search a suspect or pull over a driver. "In ambiguous situations, people are more likely to act on bias," Tyler says. "If you have a script to follow, that's more objective."

Implementing protocols to circumvent bias could be helpful in the short term. Looking ahead, changing hiring practices could be an effective way to reduce racial disparities, says Corey, whose research focuses on selecting new officers. His research explores the cognitive characteristics that make a person more likely to resist the automatic effects of implicit bias.

For example, he points to research by B. Keith Payne, PhD, at Ohio State University, who found that people with poor executive control were more likely to express automatic race biases as behavior discrimination (*Journal of Personality and Social Psychology*, 2005). By hiring police candidates who already possess qualities such as greater executive control, Corey says, "we can select police officers less likely to require cognitive reshaping."

Rebuilding Community

Reducing and circumventing bias is one way to chip away at the disparities in how police treat black civilians. Another is to focus on the positive. Many departments are taking a fresh look at community policing, in which police and community members collaborate to rebuild trust and build safer neighborhoods.

Experts say efforts to reach across racial lines to build ties with community members could help to reduce disparities. Community policing efforts might include town meetings, polls and surveys, sitting down with interest groups and foot patrols to increase an officer's interactions with the neighborhood.

It's hardly a radical concept. "In the past, an officer used to walk a beat. They'd get out of their car, get to know people," says Dovidio. "When you don't have those personal experiences, you tend to treat people in a homogeneous way."

But over the last several decades that policing style has fallen out of favor as police have taken a hard line on minor offenses in an effort to reduce crime rates. "Policing in last 30 years in

America has focused on a mission of crime control," says Tyler. Departments began adopting procedures such as New York City's controversial "stop-and-frisk" program, which encouraged officers to stop pedestrians and search them for weapons and contraband. Columbia University statistician Andrew Gelman, PhD, and colleagues reported that the program had the effect of disproportionately targeting black and Hispanic citizens, even after controlling for race-specific crime rates in the various precincts (*Journal of the American Statistical Association*, 2007).

Critics say such programs drive a wedge between police and community members, eroding trust. That lack of trust could be particularly problematic when layered on top of implicit racial stereotypes. "Effective policing requires the cooperation of the community. If the community doesn't trust you, they won't give you info to help you do your job," says Dovidio. "If you can create a sense of being on the same team, having the same goals, it makes policing more effective."

Writing on the Wall

As citizens continue to demand change, police departments increasingly understand the importance of taking action, says Tyler. "I think many see the writing on the wall. It's in their interest to get ahead of the curve to prepare and reduce the likelihood of these politically damaging events."

Major police departments such as Chicago and New York City are making efforts to take action based on evidence, he says. And the Department of Justice recently issued a final report from the President's Task Force on 21st Century Policing that drew from research including the psychological literature, he says. "On the highest level, national leaders in policing are making an effort to do things based in research," Tyler says.

As such efforts continue, psychologists can help by studying disparities, developing new interventions and testing what works in the real world.

Glaser, for instance, is a co-investigator on the National Justice Database, a project at the Center for Policing Equity with funding from the National Science Foundation. The project team is studying use-of-force data to identify the variations in policies, practices and culture that could predict excessive force. "Data analysis doesn't solve problems on its own, but it helps to point to solutions," he says.

Dovidio adds that to be most effective, psychologists might take a hard look at their preconceived ideas about law enforcement. "If more psychologists understood how policing operates and the challenges that police face, we could do a lot in terms of creating partnerships for effective training and applications of psychological theory," he says.

> "When citizens feel heard and
> responded to, especially in contentious
> moments and in moments of
> enforcement, trust is built. Citizens
> are more likely to willingly cooperate
> and comply because they feel engaged
> with instead of engaged against."

Insight Policing Can Build Bridges

Megan Price and Bruce A. Blitman

In the following viewpoint, an interview with Megan Price conducted by Bruce A. Blitman, Prices argues that insight policing, a method of conflict resolution in which officers are trained to manage conflicts with civilians, can result in stronger trust between the police and the communities they serve. Insight policing requires officers to empathize and recognize in themselves the emotions and reactions displayed by the citizens they come into contact with. The author contends that such skills allow officers to deescalate potentially problematic encounters before they can happen. Using empathy and respect as a starting point is an encouraging step toward building bridges between the police and the public. Price is Director of the Insight Conflict Resolution Program in the School for Conflict Analysis and Resolution at George Mason University. Blitman is a longtime Mediator and Attorney with a solo practice near Fort Lauderdale, Florida.

As you read, consider the following questions:

1. What is the difference between Insight Policing and mediation?
2. Which police departments have been trained in Insight Policing, according to the author?
3. How long does a basic training course in Insight Policing take, according to the viewpoint?

Recent events in Baltimore, Maryland; Ferguson, Missouri, and elsewhere have brought national attention to the connections among police practices, violence and community progress. How can police and communities stop entrenched patterns of conflict? In this interview, Megan Price (MP), Director of the Insight Conflict Resolution Program at George Mason University's School for Conflict Analysis and Resolution, and Bruce A. Blitman (BAB), longtime mediator and Florida Bar member, discuss Insight Policing and the innovative ways in which it can improve police-community relations for the safety of the public.

1. BAB: What is Insight Policing?

MP: Insight Policing is a community-based, problem-solving, communication skill set for officers of all ranks. It is based on the principles of Insight Conflict Analysis and Resolution that recognize that conflict behavior—those fight, flight, freeze things we do when we feel threatened and choose to defend ourselves— is often at the base of criminal behavior, whether that criminal behavior is violent assault, petty theft or noncompliance with a police officer. At the same time, Insight Policing skills help officers recognize and temper their own impulses toward conflict behavior, so they can maintain a controlled and engaged presence with community members that doesn't escalate. What is unique about Insight Policing skills is that they position officers to identify, deescalate, understand and productively manage conflict behavior in civilian encounters, thereby enhancing trust and legitimacy.

2. BAB: What are the origins of Insight Policing? Why was it developed?

MP: Insight Policing was developed through a grant from the Bureau of Justice Assistance (BJA) and in collaboration with the Memphis, TN and Lowell, MA police departments in an effort to help police departments get ahead of the persistent challenge of retaliatory community violence. At the time—2011—crime rates were falling across the country, but retaliatory violence was staying the same. Departments were finding themselves struggling to prevent it and instead left to pick up its pieces. Given that retaliation is inherently action taken in the context of conflict, we were asked to weigh-in on the problem as conflict resolution experts. What we found confirmed what much of research has shown, that retaliatory violence is linked to a more systemic conflict over police legitimacy. Police, therefore, have a particular responsibility to rebuild legitimacy with communities experiencing high incidence of retaliatory violence. This is an extraordinarily difficult task, however, because there is a baseline of conflict and mistrust. Being able to understand how we operate in conflict, however, helps officers overcome it and strengthens their relationships with communities, even as they enforce the law.

3. BAB: How do you adapt Insight Policing skills to police- civilian encounters?

MP: Officers trained in Insight Policing are able to recognize both in themselves and in others when behavior is conflict behavior—what the Insight approach defines as a decision to defend against an anticipated threat. When an officer can recognize that, he can become curious about it and ask targeted Insight questions that elicit the threat and defense at the root of the behavior. Simply asking these questions deescalates mounting tension, induces the citizen to reflect on what they are doing and why, yields important information for the officer to help him or her determine the best course of action, and allows the officer to engage with the citizen in terms of the citizen's own decision making. This fosters the key components of procedural justice—citizen voice, respect, neutrality and trust, which enhance officer legitimacy.

4. BAB: How does Insight Policing differ from Mediation and other traditional forms of police responses to conflict situations?

MP: Insight Policing differs from mediation in that officers employ it in their direct interactions with citizens rather than as third parties. They notice signs of conflict behavior and get curious about it in order to reveal what is motivating it. It is different from traditional forms of police response in that it commands and controls through engagement, communication, understanding, and curiosity, rather than through force.

5. BAB: What police departments are utilizing Insight Policing today?

MP: To date select officers in Memphis, TN, Lowell, MA and Montclair, NJ have been trained in Insight Policing.

6. BAB: What can you tell us about the effectiveness of Insight Policing in these departments and communities? What responses and reactions have you received from police? What responses and reactions have you received from civilians and civic leaders?

MP: Evaluation surveys show that 80% of officers trained in Insight Policing say that Insight Policing has enhanced their ability to deescalate the feelings of threat citizens have in their encounters with police officers and that animate conflict between citizens. Officers report that with Insight Policing they have a more effective command presence without the use of force, that they are making fewer preventable arrests (arrests for crimes against a responding officer, like failure to comply), that they are getting more cooperation and compliance from community members, that they are building better cases with better information, that they are able to help community members access resources they need, that they have better rapport with community members, that they can better control their own defensiveness and anger in community encounters where they feel challenged, that they feel good at the end of their day, and that they performed their jobs with integrity. These findings show the promise of Insight Policing. However, it is still a new development in the policing and conflict resolution fields, and more evaluation is needed, particularly among citizens and civic leaders who are on the receiving end of officers' Insight Policing skills.

7. BAB: What "Insight Policing" strategies and techniques can police use to gain the trust and confidence of the citizens in the communities they serve?

MP: Using Insight Policing skills like "noticing" conflict behavior and asking "curious questions" to elicit the threat and defense motivating conflict behavior positions officers to engage with a citizen on his or her own terms and address their concerns head on. When citizens feel heard and responded to, especially in contentious moments and in moments of enforcement, trust is built. Citizens are more likely to willingly cooperate and comply because they feel engaged with instead of engaged against.

8. BAB: What are the benefits of using Insight Policing techniques and principles?

MP: Insight Policing skills enhance officers' communication skills with both self-awareness and empathy when it comes to recognizing and dealing effectively with conflict. Insight Policing skills help officers deescalate contentious encounters with civilians, engage with civilians in a procedurally just way, and make targeted and precise enforcement decisions, thereby building trust and legitimacy, and strengthening their connection to the community.

9. BAB: Can you share a "real life" example of how Insight Policing can change the dynamics of an encounter between police and civilians?

MP: Certainly, I have many examples from all kinds of policing encounters. It is interesting, because the stories officers have told me include times when they have used Insight Policing skills to get a handle on their own conflict behavior as well as when they have used the skills to deescalate the conflict behavior of a community member.

10. BAB: Can you start with an example of an officer recognizing his or her own conflict behavior?

MP: An officer in Memphis once described to me how Insight policing made a difference in the way he handled himself during a routine traffic stop. The officer pulled the car over for a traffic violation, and when he came up to the car he saw that the driver was a big man, probably 6'4" and 300 pounds. If his size wasn't intimidating enough, the man began yelling at the officer: "You're always writing tickets! There are other crimes being committed! You all need to be working towards that, not coming after me!" The officer remarked that in the past, he would have taken the man's aggression as a sign of disrespect toward his role as a police officer, and he would have called for additional cars. However, he noticed this response in himself as his own conflict behavior. If he acted on it, he realized, he would be escalating the situation. He told me that he realized that bringing more officers on to the scene just because he was offended would have put the man at a disadvantage and made him uneasy—which before Insight Policing training might well have been the point: to show the man that the officer was the one with the power. But how would it have ended? Recognizing his impulse as conflict behavior, though, the officer changed his mind. He decided, in his words, "to deal with this on a one on one level, and keep it to a moderate tone." As the officer reported, "it ended up working out real well."

11. BAB: How about an example where an officer deescalates the conflict behavior of a community member?

MP: In an example from Montclair—this comes from a school resource officer who works with kids in the high school—a student was angry and yelling and lashing out at the Vice Principal. The officer intervened. She didn't grab the student or pull him away, instead, she noticed his conflict behavior, and said, "I can see you are really mad at the Vice Principal." And he said, "Yes, I am." He started going off about the Vice Principal, but the officer stayed curious about the conflict behavior as the Insight approach suggests. She refocused the student by asking, "What is it about what the Vice Principal is doing that is making you so angry?" And according to her, the student just stopped. She could see that the question caught him off guard. She had been genuinely curious about what he was experiencing, and he told her, "No one has asked me that question, not even once, they're just asking me 'what's wrong?' and telling me to calm down." Clearly he was relieved to be wondered about in this way. The officer's question calmed him down, and to answer it, he had to think. This allowed him and the school resource officer to have a conversation. It turned out that the student was upset not because he was in trouble or because he was caught out of class, but because the Vice Principal for various reasons had promised him previously that security would not touch him, and in this instance she had instructed them to. He was reacting because he felt that she had let him down and broken a promise. Being able to communicate that deescalated an escalating situation. It put him, the school resource officer, security and the Vice Principal on the same communication plane. From there, they were able to address the issue that had gotten him in trouble in the first place, without it spiraling any further out of control.

In a more dangerous example, a Memphis officer detailed to serve a warrant on a man wanted in connection with murder told me about an experience using Insight Policing. While looking for the man, the officer reported that he and his partner came across the suspect's brothers. As the officer put it, the brothers "were real uncooperative with us." However, when the officer recognized the refusal to cooperate, not just as obstructionist, but as conflict behavior—where they were defending against some kind of a threat—he used his Insight Policing skills to ask about what made them not want to cooperate. The Insight question opened the brothers up. They were willing to tell the officer why they did not want to talk to him. What they said was that they had had bad experiences with police in the past, where the police arrested them without hearing them out, without taking the time to find out what was going on. They thought this situation would be the same. But by wondering about their concerns and by hearing what they were saying, the officer was able to defuse the brothers' concern that they were about to be arrested. And as a result, the brothers changed their minds about being aggressively uncooperative. As the officer put it to me, he was able to "talk to them and win their trust over so that they eventually turned their own brother in for the murders that he [was under investigation for]." The officer expressed amazement that the brothers were willing to bring him and his partner directly to their brother, and that when they did, the suspect willingly surrendered. There was no fight and no struggle. The officer stressed that this "kind of cooperation doesn't happen very often. Not unless you really listen to the story." His Insight policing skills had helped him do that.

12. BAB: Where can we find more examples of officers using Insight Policing skills?

MP: I have a lot of other stories published in an article I co-authored called "Insight Policing and the Role of the Civilian in Police Accountability" in *Clearinghouse Review* from the Shriver Center on Poverty Law.

13. BAB: Can you tell us about the Insight Policing training process at your university? Who can attend? Who should attend? How long is the training course? Where and when is it offered? Do you have any other details about the program?

MP: Insight Policing can be requested by any department across the country just by contacting our office at insight@gmu.edu or through our website, insightconflictresolution.org. Insight Policing trainers train on-site to deliver a hands on, experiential course to officers through exercises and role-play. For this reason, the Insight Conflict Resolution Program likes to work with a department to tailor the training to their specific needs and contexts. An

8-hour basic course is available, as is a more intensive 16-24 hour course that includes certification. An instructor training course is currently in development.

14. BAB: What are your goals and visions for the future of Insight Policing?

MP: My ultimate goal is to make Insight Policing available to officers in departments nationwide so that officers have the communication skills they need to engage with community members in ways that uphold the integrity of their commitment to the public as they enforce the law and keep communities safe.

15. BAB: Do you have any other reflections about Insight Policing you would like to share with our audience?

MP: The whole nation is crying out to mend the conflict between the police and the public that has been building since the death of Michael Brown. We are all devastated by the violence coming from both directions and are looking for a way to stop it and to change the prevailing experience of police as executors of force. Insight Policing is a community-oriented, problem-solving, communication tactic that can help do that. It can reengage officers and civilians in procedurally just ways that build trust and bolster police legitimacy.

Periodical and Internet Sources Bibliography

The following articles have been selected to supplement the diverse views presented in this chapter.

Affinity "The truth about Black Lives Matter and black-on-black crime," Affinity, July 13, 2017. http://affinitymagazine. us/2017/07/13/the-truth-about-black-lives-matter-and-black-on-black-crime/

Conor Friedersdorf "Should Black Lives Matter focus on black-on-black murders," *The Atlantic*, October 7, 2015. https://www. theatlantic.com

Josh Hafner "Why Black Lives Matter doesn't focus on 'black-on-black' crime," *USA Today*, July 27, 2016. https://www.usatoday. com/story/news/nation-now/2016/07/27/why-doesnt-black-lives-matter-doesnt-focus-talk-about-black-black-crime/87609692/

Michael Harriot "Why we never talk about black-on-black crime: An answer to white America's most pressing question," The Root, October 3, 2017. http://www.theroot.com/why-we-never-talk-about-black-on-black-crime-an-answer-1819092337

Jamiles Lartey "'Demolish that lie': James Forman Jr. takes on Black Lives Matter backlash," *The Guardian*, April 29, 2017. https:// www.theguardian.com/us-news/2017/apr/29/james-forman-jr-locking-up-our-own-black-on-black-crime

Barbara Reynolds "I was a civil rights activist in the 1960s. But it's hard for me to get behind Black Lives Matter," *Washington Post*, August 24, 2015. https://www.washingtonpost.com/posteverything/wp/2015/08/24/i-was-a-civil-rights-activist-in-the-1960s-but-its-hard-for-me-to-get-behind-black-lives-matter/?utm_term=.c748b1135f2c

The Economist "The misplaced arguments against Black Lives Matter," August 18, 2017. http://www.economist.com/blogs/economist-explains/2017/08/economist-explains-15

Janice Williams "Majority of Americans have unfavorable view of Black Lives Matter, say black crime is a top concern," *Newsweek*, August 3, 2017. http://www.newsweek.com/black-lives-matter-protests-police-646050

OPPOSING
VIEWPOINTS®
SERIES

Black Lives Matter: Peaceful Protesters or Fermenters of Violence?

Chapter Preface

T here is no denying the visibility of Black Lives Matter. Its members have been seen prominently in protest marches in recent years, including a few that have turned violent. They have been outspoken in events organized by themselves or others that rail against perceived police brutality and racism. They have also played roles in demonstrations against the rights of white supremacists and white nationalists to speak on college campuses.

Most of those that express opinions in the following chapter on whether Black Lives Matter is a group that promotes violence or simply embraces the right of all Americans to peacefully protest do not generally lump all its members into one category. Only the irrational on either side of the issue claim that all BLM members push for violent change or that none of them do. It is generally understood that the truth lies somewhere in between. Though views backing and criticizing Black Lives Matter are represented here, one can argue that few of them are so extreme as to be foolhardy.

There are exceptions One popular modern-day expression is "perception is reality." Such could not be further from the truth in studying the motivation of Black Lives Matter. Folks that perceive extremism on either side, such as those that signed a petition that defines BLM as a terrorist organization, prove that some people use their fears and prejudices rather than their logic in their analysis. Neither can those that favorably compare the impact of Black Lives Matter to the civil rights movement of the 1950s and 1960s, which legally overturned centuries of impacted racism and discrimination in the United States, be taken seriously. Only through unbiased study can one form the worthy opinion that are most prevalent among the viewpoints that make up this chapter.

> "No matter what the issue, no matter
> what the facts, the Left advances a
> relentless, hate-filled narrative that
> America is irredeemably evil and
> must be destroyed as soon as possible.
> The BLM movement is only the latest
> but perhaps most dangerous variant
> on this divisive theme."

Black Lives Matter Is Supported by Communism

James Simpson

In the following viewpoint, James Simpson argues that international communism is the force behind the Black Lives Matter movement to ferment discord and violence in America. This is a similar contention to one used to smear the civil rights movement of the 1950s and 1960s. Simpson claims here that BLM is funded greatly by what he defines as radical left-wing organizations. Simpson's assertion leaves open the criticism that he does not give enough credit to Black Lives Matter and its supporters as well-meaning activists with minds and motivations of their own. Simpson is an economist, journalist, and former White House budget analyst.

"Reds Exploiting Blacks: The Roots of Black Lives Matter," by James Simpson, Accuracy in Media, January 12, 2016. Reprinted by permission.

As you read, consider the following questions:

1. What hard facts does the author provide to support his claim that socialists and communists are behind Black Lives Matter?

2. How does the author use a claim about the life of a younger Barack Obama to make his point?

3. What evidence might a reader cite in the article that the author is against gay rights?

The Black Lives Matter movement (BLM) casts itself as a spontaneous uprising born of inner city frustration, but is, in fact, the latest and most dangerous face of a web of well-funded communist/socialist organizations that have been agitating against America for decades. Its agitation has provoked police killings and other violence, lawlessness and unrest in minority communities throughout the U.S. If allowed to continue, that agitation could devolve into anarchy and civil war. The BLM crowd appears to be spoiling for just such an outcome.

Nevertheless, BLM appears to be exercising considerable leverage over the Democratic Party, in part by pressuring and intimidating Democratic candidates such as Hillary Clinton and Bernie Sanders (VT) into embracing their cause. The movement could also assist President Obama's exploitation of racial divisions in society beyond his final term in office.

This report examines in detail, for the first time, how communist groups have manipulated the cause of Black Lives Matter, and how money from liberal foundations has made it all possible.

Leftist Origins

Exploiting blacks to promote Marxist revolution is an old tactic. The late Larry Grathwohl, former FBI informant in the Weather Underground, understood from personal experience how white communists exploited blacks and other minority groups. He said that Weather Underground terrorists Bill Ayers and Bernardine

Dohrn regarded Barack Obama, whose political career they sponsored, as a tool—a puppet—to use against white America. Obama's legacy at home will certainly include more racial division.

BLM launched in 2013 with a Twitter hashtag, #BlackLivesMatter, after neighborhood watchman George Zimmerman was acquitted in the Trayvon Martin killing. Radical Left activists Alicia Garza, Patrisse Cullors and Opal Tometi claim credit for the slogan and hashtag. Following the Michael Brown shooting in August 2014, Dream Defenders, an organization led by Working Families Party (ACORN) activist and Occupy Wall Street anarchist Nelini Stamp, popularized the phrase "Hands Up–Don't Shoot!" which has since become BLM's widely recognized slogan.

Garza, Cullors and Tometi all work for front groups of the Freedom Road Socialist Organization (FRSO), one of the four largest radical Left organizations in the country. The others are the Communist Party USA (CPUSA), Democratic Socialists of America (DSA), and the Committees of Correspondence for Democracy and Socialism (CCDS). Nelini Stamp's ACORN—now rebranded under a variety of different names—works with all four organizations, and Dream Defenders is backed by the Service Employees International Union (SEIU), the ACLU, the Southern Poverty Law Center and others.

FRSO is a hereditary descendant of the New Communist Movement, which was inspired by Mao and the many communist revolutions throughout the world in the 1960s and 1970s. FRSO split into two separate groups in 1999, FRSO/Fight Back and FRSO/OSCL (Freedom Road Socialist Organization/Organizacion Socialista del Camino para la Libertad). Black Lives Matter and its founders are allied with the latter group. Future references to FRSO in this article refer to FRSO/OSCL.

FRSO is comprised of dozens of groups. The radical Left model is based on alliances of many organizations that are working on separate issues but dedicated ultimately to the same thing: overthrowing our society in order to replace it with a hardcore socialist (read communist) one.

The goal is to present the appearance of a formidable mass of organizations. Some are large, but many are little more than a website or Facebook page. When necessary, they can all come together to promote the cause du jour. The deaths of Trayvon Martin, Michael Brown and others were mere pretexts for socialist agitation. The real enemy is "the system." This is why the BLM crowd denies the facts of those cases. As Stamp has said, "we are actually trying to change the capitalist system we have today because it's not working for any of us." BLM is one of many projects undertaken by the FRSO. Except for the website, blacklivesmatter.com, there is no actual organization. The website implicitly acknowledges this, describing #BlackLivesMatter as "an online forum intended to build connections between Black people and our allies to fight anti-Black racism, to spark dialogue among Black people, and to facilitate the types of connections necessary to encourage social action and engagement."

FRSO membership is disproportionately represented by blacks, gays and women, and self-consciously emphasizes those issues. Garza, who penned a "Herstory" of BLM, is a "queer," black veteran activist involved in numerous FRSO organizations. Her resumé includes:

- Special projects director, National Domestic Workers Alliance (NDWA)
- Executive Director, People Organized to Win Employment Rights (POWER)
- Board member, School of Unity and Liberation (SOUL)
- 2011 Board Chair, Right to the City Alliance (RTTC)

Cullors describes herself as a "working class, queer, black woman." She claims the country killed her father, a drug addict. At a 2015 Netroots Nation conference, Cullors led chants shouting, "If I die in police custody, burn everything down… rise the f--- up! That is the only way m-----f-----s like you will listen!" Cullors founded and directs Dignity and Power Now (DPN), which claims to seek "dignity and power of incarcerated people, their families, and communities."

Cullors was trained by Eric Mann, a former Weather Underground leader who exhorts followers to become "anti-racist, anti-imperialist" activists. Mann runs another FRSO front, the Labor/Community Strategy Center. Like most professional leftists, he makes good money—over $225,000 annually—living in "the system" he advocates destroying.

Tometi is the daughter of illegal aliens from Nigeria. While in college, she worked for the ACLU defending illegal aliens against "vigilantes" opposed to illegal immigration. She is currently the executive director of Black Alliance for Just Immigration (BAJI).

The Funding

FRSO/BLM organizations are generously supported by a universe of wealthy foundations. Some, like those employing BLM founders Garza and Tometi, receive money directly. Others, like Cullors' DPN, are financed by organizations designed specifically to underwrite the activities of others. Amounts reflect donations received over approximately the past decade.

Major NDWA Foundation Donors

Ben & Jerry's	$30,000
Ford	$1,910,000
Kellogg	$250,000
Marguerite Casey	$450,000
Nathan Cummings	$500,000
Oak	$489,500
Rockefeller	$134,000
Soros Funds	$1,344,846
Surdna	$235,000
Other	$777,550
Total	**$6,120,896**

NDWA (Garza)—2013 revenues were $5.5 million. The NDWA board includes two members of CASA de Maryland, the Illegals' version of ACORN. CASA also received a grant from NDWA in 2013, as did the radical Left Institute for Policy Studies. NDWA receives funding from the following foundations:

POWER (Garza)—2013 revenues were $456,676, including $92,173 in government grants. POWER evolved from the now defunct communist group STORM (Standing Together to Organize a Revolutionary Movement). Obama's former "Green Jobs Czar" the self-described communist, Van Jones, served on STORM's board.

Major POWER Foundation Donors

Akonadi	$120,000
Ben & Jerry's	$25,000
Ford	$1,325,000
Marguerite Casey	$300,000
Soros Funds	$600,000
Surdna	$400,000
Tides	$165,000
Other	$402,500
Total	**$3,337,500**

RTTC (Garza)—2013 revenues were $248,190. RTTC is a nationwide network of activist organizations that resists the gentrification of inner cities because it displaces "low-income people, people of color, marginalized LGBTQ communities, and youths of color..."

Major RTTC Foundation Donors

Akonadi	$120,000
Ben & Jerry's	$25,000
Ford	$1,325,000
Marguerite Casey	$300,000
Soros Funds	$600,000
Surdna	$400,000
Tides	$165,000
Other	$402,500
Total	**$3,337,500**

SOUL (Garza)—Despite its small size (2013 revenues at $110,304), SOUL claims to have trained 679 organizers in 2013.

Major SOUL Foundation Donors

Akonadi	$322,500
Heinz	$255,000
Hill Snowden	$142,500
Rockefeller	$210,000
San Francisco	$105,000
Surdna	$460,000
Tides	$298,000
Other	$290,750
Total	**$2,083,750**

BAJI (Tometi)—2013 revenues were $321,570. This modest organization only lists two full-time staff, yet receives support from many recognizable foundations.

Major BAJI Foundation Donors

Ben & Jerry's	$10,000
Kellogg	$75,000
Marguerite Casey	$337,500
San Francisco	$75,600
Soros Funds	$200,000
Other	$175,000
Total	**$873,100**

Cullors' DPN is underwritten by Community Partners, a Los Angeles based non-profit with a $24 million budget (including $4 million in government grants) that fiscally sponsors non-profits. It is not an FRSO organization.

Advancement Project (AP)—an FRSO group that funds a variety of radical causes. AP sees America as a racist, oppressive nation and, according to Discover the Networks, "works to organize 'communities of color' into politically cohesive units while disseminating its leftist worldviews and values as broadly as possible by way of a sophisticated communications department." Its 2013 revenues were $11.3 million.

Major AP Foundation Donors

California Endowment	$7,354,814
Ford	$8,466,000
Hewlett	$2,465,000
James Irvine	$2,542,500
Kellogg	$3,000,000
Rockefeller	$2,450,000
Soros Funds	$8,565,275
Tides	$1,260,540
Vanguard	$1,691,000
All others	$16,777,157
Total	**$54,572,286**

Movement Strategy Center (MSC)—also facilitates funding, development and advancement of FRSO organizations. Its 2013 revenues were $7.5 million, including $156,032 in government grants.

Major MSC Foundation Donors

Akonadi	$1,094,500
Ben & Jerry's	$60,000
California Endowment	$2,325,862
Ford	$1,762,500
Robert Wood Johnson	$378,750
Rockefeller	$398,000
San Francisco Foundation	$551,206
Soros Funds	$1,100,000
Surdna	$1,445,000
Tides	$1,607,000
All others	$4,541,469
Total	**$15,264,287**

The Return of Van Jones

Mainstream funders have helped fund BLM as well. For example, United Way has partnered with A&E and iHeartMedia to create Shining the Light Advisors, a committee of "nationally known experts and leaders in racial and social justice," to oversee grant disbursements. These "advisors" include such radicals as Van Jones, Advancement Project co-director Judith Browne Dianis, and Rinku Sen, president of the Applied Research Center (ARC).

BLM's mission includes a kitchen sink of favored radical Left causes, including support of poverty elimination programs, prison deinstitutionalization, illegal immigration and gay rights. Highlighting FRSO's orientation toward gay blacks, it describes how "Black, queer and trans folks bear a unique burden from a hetero-patriarchal society that disposes of us like garbage and simultaneously fetishizes us and profits off of us, and that is state violence."

Its wide network of affiliates and partner organizations like CPUSA and ACORN allows BLM to turn out large crowds. Many participate simply to protest, commit violence, loot or all three.

FRSO was prominent at the Ferguson protests and videoed the event. It has even created a Black Lives Matter button. Following are more FRSO organizations involved with BLM. (Funding estimates provided when known).

- Black Left Unity—A Marxist/Leninist organization that supports favored causes of the communist Left, including unity with Cuba, war against capitalism and Occupy Wall Street.
- Black Workers for Justice—A North Carolina-based group which claims to struggle on behalf of "oppressed nationalities," etc.
- Causa Justa/Just Cause—A Black/Latino solidarity organization allied with the Grassroots Global Justice Alliance, RTTC and others. Its 2013 revenues were $1.6 million, including $689,484 in government grants.
- Grassroots Global Justice Alliance (GGJ)—"a national alliance of US-based grassroots organizing (GRO) groups organizing to build an agenda for power for working and poor people and communities of color."
- Hands Up United—Works for "liberation of oppressed Black, Brown, and poor people through education, art, civil disobedience, advocacy, and agriculture."
- Intelligent Mischief—Their *Black Body Survival Guide* is in the works and has raised over $8,000 through IndieGoGo.
- Organization for Black Struggle (OBS)—This organization is affiliated with the CPUSA. Its website claims its allies as Black Workers for Justice and the Advancement Project. Chaired by FRSO member Montague Simmons.
- Revolutionary Student Coordinating Committee (RSCC) a militant group founded in 2012 by CUNY students. It is

networked at different U.S. colleges. This group organized the infamous pro-abortion "Hail Satan" chant at Texas capital.

- Showing Up for Racial Justice (SURJ) is a "national network of groups and individuals organizing White people for racial justice." SURJ quotes Garza saying that "We need you defecting from White supremacy and changing the narrative of White supremacy by breaking White silence."
- Strategic Concepts in Organizing and Policy Education (SCOPE)—Its 2013 revenues were $2.8 million. Led by Anthony Thigpenn, a former Black Panther and board member of the Apollo Alliance. Apollo is the secretive alliance of labor, environment and other Left activists that formulated Obama's trillion dollar "stimulus" plan. Board member Van Jones described Apollo "as sort of a grand unified field theory for progressive Left causes." It is now a project of the Blue Green Alliance.

Major SCOPE Foundation Donors

California Endowment	$3,627,037
Carnegie	$300,000
Ford	$4,860,000
Haas	$750,000
Hewlett	$1,475,000
James Irvine	$2,750,000
Marguerite Casey	$2,000,000
New World	$1,540,000
Open Society (Soros)	$650,000
Rockefeller	$705,000
Tides	$410,000
Others	$3,678,857
Total	**$22,745,894**

BLM groups have also joined with CPUSA, CCDS, DSA, SEIU, Color of Change and many others. Anarchist and top OWS organizer Lisa Fithian, who orchestrated the 1999 Seattle World Trade Organization riots, trained Ferguson protesters. Fithian says "Create crisis, because crisis is that edge where change is possible."

Fithian echoes Richard Cloward and Frances Fox Piven— creators of the infamous Cloward/Piven Crisis Strategy—who spent decades attempting to provoke ghetto blacks to riot, because "Poor people can advance only when 'the rest of society is afraid of them.'" Rasheen Aldridge, seen above meeting President Obama, was a leader of the Ferguson protests. He has participated in numerous CPUSA events in 2013, 2014 and 2015. Another prominent CPUSA member active in BLM protests is Michael McPhearson, who leads the Don't Shoot Coalition.

Carl Davidson and Pat Fry, co-chairs of CCDS, exploited the revolutionary atmosphere of the Ferguson riots to create an eight-point plan for "Left Unity" demanding "a common aspiration for socialism."

Missourians Organizing for Reform and Empowerment (MORE) is Missouri's rebranded ACORN group. It created an illustrative chart offering a snapshot of the Left's grievance agenda. Capitalism is always the problem. Socialism is always the solution.

Interestingly, MORE doesn't believe in socialism when it is footing the bill. MORE promised to pay Ferguson protesters $5,000/ month to hang out and cause trouble. But just as ACORN stiffed its employees while preaching socialist generosity, MORE stiffed the protesters.

Islamist organizations have also jumped on the BLM bandwagon, reminding us of the unholy alliance that exists between them and the radical Left. In September 2015, the Muslim Brotherhood front-group Council on American Islamic Relations (CAIR) joined BLM activists in storming California Governor Jerry Brown's office. CAIR also participated in the Ferguson protests. Meanwhile ISIS is recruiting American blacks for its cause.

CLAIMS OF TERRORISM

An official petition to the White House asking the "Black Lives Matter" movement to be formally recognised as a terrorist entity has garnered 85,000 plus signatures at time of writing, meaning it will almost certainly have to be addressed by the Obama administration.

The petition, hosted on the whitehouse.gov website, was created one day before the attack on police in Dallas, but has picked up steam in its wake.

The blurb of the petition states:

"Terrorism is defined as "the use of violence and intimidation in pursuit of political aims". This definition is the same definition used to declare ISIS and other groups, as terrorist organizations. Black Lives Matter has earned this title due to its actions in Ferguson, Baltimore, and even at a Bernie Sanders rally, as well as all over the United States and Canada. It is time for the pentagon to be consistent in its actions—and just as they rightfully declared ISIS a terror group, they must declare Black Lives Matter a terror group—on the grounds of principle, integrity, morality, and safety."

Petitions on the White House website need to reach 100,000 signatures in order to receive an official response. Consequently, at time of writing, only around 13,000 more are needed.

Of course, it is patently obvious that the Obama administration will not even consider publicly labeling any self described member of 'Black Lives Matter' as a terrorist or radical.

Already, figures within the government have refrained from connecting the shooting in Dallas, in which five police officers were murdered, with the Black Lives Matter movement, despite the fact it occurred at one of their rallies, and that the shooter identified as a member of black power groups.

Department of Homeland Security (DHS) Secretary Jeh Johnson went as far as declining to define the massacre a hate crime, and said that it is not reflective of movements like Black Lives Matter.

"At a time like this when tensions are high, in the wake of events in Dallas and Baton Rouge and Minnesota and elsewhere, it's important to remember that just as the shooter on Thursday night is not reflective of the broader movement to bring about change in police practices that any police officer who engages in excessive force is not representative of the larger law enforcement community, which with increasing frequency, reflects the community at large," Johnson said Sunday on NBC's "Meet the Press."

"Petition To Recognize 'Black Lives Matter' As A Terrorist Organization Gets 85,000 Signatures," by Steve Watson, Infowars.com, July 11, 2016.

Intellectual Genealogy of Black Lives Matter

"We must be ready to employ trickery, deceit, law-breaking, withholding and concealing truth… We can and must write in a language which sows among the masses hate, revulsion, and scorn toward those who disagree with us."

—Vladimir Lenin

That quote from the Soviet Union's first leader captures the entire essence of the Left's strategy. No matter what the issue, no matter what the facts, the Left advances a relentless, hate-filled narrative that America is irredeemably evil and must be destroyed as soon as possible. The BLM movement is only the latest but perhaps most dangerous variant on this divisive theme.

Communists use language and psychology as weapons. Their constant vilification is a form of psychological terror. It puts America and Americans on trial. The verdict is always guilty. Facts don't matter because the Left does not want to resolve the problems they complain about. They use those problems to agitate and provoke, hoping conflict becomes unavoidable—thereby creating a self-fulfilling prophecy. Their hatred is tactical.

Obama's favorite Harvard professor Derrick Bell devised Critical Race Theory, which exemplifies Lenin's strategy as applied to race. According to Discover the Networks:

> Critical race theory contends that America is permanently racist to its core, and that consequently the nation's legal structures are, by definition, racist and invalid ... members of "oppressed" racial groups are entitled—in fact obligated—to determine for themselves which laws and traditions have merit and are worth observing...

Bell's theory is in turn an innovation of Critical Theory—developed by philosophers of the communist Frankfurt School. The school was founded in Frankfurt, Germany in 1923. Its Jewish communist scholars fled Hitler's Germany in the 1930s, relocating to Columbia Teachers College in New York. Critical Theory—which discredits all aspects of Western society—rapidly infected the minds of newly-minted college professors, who then spread its poison throughout the university system. We know it today as political correctness.

White Privilege

The "racist" narrative was turbocharged with the concept of "White Privilege," the notion that whites—the dominant group in capitalist America—are irretrievably racist, sexist, homophobic, xenophobic, fill-in-the-blank-ophobic, imperialistic oppressors who exploit everyone. Whites are the only true evil in the world and should be exterminated.

The "White Skin Privilege" idea was created in 1967 by Noel Ignatiev, an acolyte of Bell and professor at Harvard's W.E.B. Du Bois Institute (Du Bois was a Communist black leader who helped found the NAACP). Ignatiev was a member of CPUSA's most radical wing, the Maoist/Stalinist Provisional Organizing Committee to Reconstitute the Marxist-Leninist Communist Party (POC). POC was the intellectual forerunner to FRSO.

Writing under the alias Noel Ignatin, Ignatiev co-authored an SDS pamphlet with fellow radical Ted Allen, titled *White Blindspot*. In 1992 he co-founded *Race Traitor: Journal of the New Abolitionism*. Its first issue coined the slogan, "Treason to whiteness is loyalty to humanity." Its stated objective was to "abolish the white race." More specifically, the *New Abolitionist* newsletter stated:

> The way to abolish the white race is to challenge, disrupt and eventually overturn the institutions and behavior patterns that reproduce the privileges of whiteness, including the schools, job and housing markets, and the criminal justice system. *The abolitionists do not limit themselves to socially acceptable means of protest, but reject in advance no means of attaining their goal* (emphasis added).

But do not be confused; "White" does not mean white. "White" in radical construction means anyone of any race, creed, nationality, color, sex, or sexual preference who embraces capitalism, free markets, limited government and American traditional culture and values. By definition, these beliefs are irredeemably evil and anyone who aligns with them is "white" in spirit and thus equally guilty of "white crimes." Ignatiev still teaches, now at the Massachusetts College of Art.

The Black Lives Matter movement carries this narrative to unprecedented heights, claiming that only whites can be racists. And while justifying violence to achieve "social justice," the movement's goal is to overthrow our society to replace it with a Marxist one. Many members of the black community would be shocked to learn that the intellectual godfathers of this movement are mostly white Communists, "queers" and leftist Democrats, intent on making blacks into cannon fodder for the revolution.

> *"They are rejecting the charismatic leadership model that has dominated black politics for the past half century, and for good reason."*

Black Lives Matter Is Breathing New Life into the Civil Rights Movement

Fredrick C. Harris

In the following viewpoint, Frederick C. Harris argues that Black Lives Matter owes a lot to the civil rights movement of the 1950s and 1960s, but that it should also learn from the mistakes of that movement. In comparing Black Lives Matter with the civil rights movement, the author contends that BLM boasts the potential to be as or more impactful, and far more wide-ranging in scope and participation. Harris is a professor of political science and director of the Center on African-American Politics and Society at Columbia University.

As you read, consider the following questions:

1. Why does the author believe that strong individual leadership will not be a necessary component of Black Lives Matter?
2. What role does the author cite for social media in the BLM movement?
3. What active 1960s organization does the author see as a model for Black Lives Matter?

"The Next Civil Rights Movement?" by Fredrick C. Harris, Dissent Magazine, Summer 2015. Reprinted with permission of the University of Pennsylvania Press.

Kareem Jackson, a St. Louis hip-hop artist who goes by the name Tef Poe, was interviewed this February by a BBC talk show host about why the Black Lives Matter movement was necessary. A leader in the organization Hands Up United, which was founded in the wake of Michael Brown's murder, Poe explained: "One of the negligent areas of the civil rights movement is that we did not move the moral compass of racism to the right direction."

Though the 1960s movement addressed the civil and political rights that were denied to black people—access and use of public accommodations, the right to vote, and ensuring fair employment and housing opportunities—it did not directly confront the racialized degradation black people endured, and many continue to endure, at the hands of the police. What the Black Lives Matter protests have done, however, is not only put police reform on the policy agenda but demanded that American society reconsider how it values black lives.

Tef Poe had not been directly involved in politics until Brown's death. He was a struggling hip-hop artist who occasionally wrote a column for the *Riverfront Times*, an independent newspaper in St. Louis. One day, while checking his Instagram account, Poe noticed a post that shook him. It was a photograph of Brown's stepfather holding up a hand-written sign that read simply, "My unarmed child has been murdered by the Ferguson police." As he watched the wave of anger, disgust, and disbelief mount on his social media feed within hours of the shooting, Tef Poe knew he had to go to Ferguson. This is how he—along with legions of people across the country—was transformed into an activist, not just concerned with civil and political rights but with black humanity.

The protests that have erupted since the deaths of Brown and other casualties of police brutality have been extraordinary. Seemingly out of nowhere, a multiracial, multigenerational movement asserting black humanity in response to racist police killings and vigilante violence has ripped across the country. The police brutality and killings are not, to be sure, new; the emerging movement against them, however, is. The upsurge in anti-racist organizing is a break from what we normally consider black activism in the United States. Each periodic wave of activism for the last half century—whether centered on electoral politics or protests—has traced its lineage to the "golden age" of the 1960s. But while there is a great deal of nostalgia in these comparisons, core activists of the Black Lives Matter movement have been quick to remind us that this current wave of protest "is not your grandmamma's civil rights movement."

In a purely tactical sense, that assessment is correct. The movement's use of technology to mobilize hundreds of thousands of people through social media is light years away from the labor that was once required to mobilize black people and their allies during the 1960s or even a few years ago. Jo Ann Robinson of the all-black Women's Political Council in Montgomery, for instance, spent hours using a hand-driven mimeograph machine to crank out over 52,000 leaflets that announced a mass protest after Rosa Parks's arrest in 1955.

Today, social media—particularly Twitter—can reach individuals throughout the nation and across the world in milliseconds, drastically slashing the time it takes to organize protests. As a recent *New York Times Magazine* spread noted, through Twitter, core Black Lives Matter activists like Johnetta Elzie and DeRay Mckesson, who are based in St. Louis, now have the ability to frame events and direct the actions of hundreds of thousands of people across the nation at their fingertips. Not only is social media a tool for mobilization, but the intense reporting on police brutality via social media also influences print and television coverage, which means that attention to such incidents has multiplied. Twitter and Facebook have, in this way, become documentary tools for Black Lives Matter activists, a way for them to become citizen journalists capturing the protests and police responses in almost real time. Indeed, for this reason, the spontaneity and the intensity of Black Lives Matter is more akin to other recent movements—Occupy Wall Street and the explosive protests in Egypt and Brazil—than 1960s activism.

A President's Words

President Barack Obama called Sunday for greater tolerance, respect and understanding from police officers toward the people they take an oath to protect as well as from individuals who think the police are too heavy handed and intolerant, particularly toward people of color.

"I'd like all sides to listen to each other," Obama said.

It was the fourth straight day that Obama has commented on a series of distressing events back home: the fatal shootings by police of black men in Louisiana and Minnesota, and a sniper attack that killed five police officers and wounded seven in Dallas.

The president alluded to the controversial Black Lives Matter protests against police brutality that have occurred across the country, defending the movement as crucial to the preservation of free speech. "One of the great things about America is that individual citizens and groups of citizens can petition their government, can protest, can speak truth to power. And that is sometimes messy and controversial. But because of that ability to protest and engage in free speech, America over time has gotten better. We've all benefitted from that."

He mentioned other "contentious" movements that occurred throughout the nation's history, comparing them to the recent protests: "The abolition movement was contentious. The effort for women to get the right to vote was contentious and messy. There were times when activists might have engaged in rhetoric that was overheated, and occasionally counterproductive, but the point was to raise issues so that we as a society could grapple with them. The same was true with the Civil Rights movement and the Union movement and the environmental movement and the anti-war movement during Vietnam. And I think what you're seeing now is part of that long standing tradition."

Obama noted, however, that violence against police does "a disservice to the cause." He repeated that the vast majority of U.S. police officers are doing a good job.

"Obama Compares Black Lives Matter Protests to Abolition, Women's Suffrage Movements," by Carly Hoilman, TheBlaze, Inc., July 10, 2016.

Similarly, images of police violence are helping put pressure on municipal police departments to address these issues. Unlike the images of brutality that sparked outrage in the past—photographs of lynch victims hanging from trees during the age of Jim Crow or newspaper images of brutalized black bodies lying in a coroner's office—we are now able to witness and document police violence as it happens. Videos from handheld phones and surveillance cameras have shown Marlene Pinnock being beaten by a California highway patrol officer, the ambush police shooting of John Crawford at a Walmart in Ohio, the chokehold death of Eric Garner in Staten Island, the drive-by police shooting of twelve-year-old Tamir Rice in Cleveland, and the crippling condition of Freddie Gray as he was arrested in Baltimore, before he eventually died.

But it is not only technological and tactical differences that separate Black Lives Matter activists from their civil rights predecessors. When activists remind us that the Black Lives Matter movement is different from the civil rights movement, they are making a conscious decision to avoid mistakes from the past. They are rejecting the charismatic leadership model that has dominated black politics for the past half century, and for good reason.

This older model is associated with Martin Luther King and the clergy-based, male-centered hierarchal structure of the organization he led, the Southern Christian Leadership Conference. In the ensuing years, this charismatic model has been replicated, most notably through organizations like Jesse Jackson's Rainbow PUSH Coalition and Al Sharpton's National Action Network, but also by hundreds of other locally based activist organizations across the country. But Black Lives Matter activists today recognize that granting decision-making power to an individual or a handful of individuals poses a risk to the durability of a movement. Charismatic leaders can be co-opted by powerful interests, place their own self-interest above that of the collective, be targeted by government repression, or even be assassinated, as were Martin Luther King and Malcolm X. The dependence of movements on charismatic leaders can therefore weaken them, even lead to their collapse.

Instead, core activists of the Black Lives Matter movement have insisted on a group-centered model of leadership, rooted in ideas of participatory democracy. The movement has modeled itself after the Student Nonviolent Coordinating Committee (SNCC), the 1960s organization that helped black Americans gain legal access to public spaces and the right to vote. Black Lives Matter organizers also operate on the principle that no one person or group of individuals should speak for or make decisions on behalf of the movement. They believe, as the legendary civil rights activist Ella Baker believed, that "strong people don't need strong leaders."

In some ways, the new tools of technology—particularly social media and especially Twitter—have facilitated the emergence of just such a bottom-up insurgency led by ordinary people, and have displaced the top-down approach of old guard civil rights organizations. But this model has also been adopted by design. For many young black Americans, leaders like Jesse Jackson and Al Sharpton, as well as heads of civil rights organizations such as the NAACP and the National Urban League, are no longer seen as the gatekeepers of the movement's ideals or the leaders who must broker the interests of black communities with the state or society. Additionally, with the exception of Al Sharpton's National Action Network, which has represented families of victims but has been less effective accomplishing police and prison reform, policing and mass incarceration have not been aggressively pursued by these more traditional organizations. And none, certainly, have adopted the disruptive protest tactics—the street marches, die-ins, bridge and tunnel blockades, and the intense publicity campaigns—that have helped Black Lives Matter force these issues onto the national political agenda.

Unlike the civil rights movement, the focus of Black Lives Matter—on policing in black and brown communities, on dismantling mass incarceration—is also being articulated less as a demand for specific civil or political rights, and more as a broader claim for "black humanity." This insistence on black humanity has repeatedly been used by Black Lives Matter activists as a catalyst for political action. "If you can see a dead black boy lie in the street for four and a half hours and that doesn't make you angry, then you lack humanity," said Ashley Yates, a Ferguson activist and co-founder of Millennial Activists United, at a rally last October. Evoking humanity is used to express communal anger against police brutality, but also to mobilize those who aren't acting. Yates explained further:

> And at the very core of this is humanity—Black Lives Matter. We matter. We matter. Black lives matter because they are lives. Because we are human. Because we eat. Because we breathe. Because he [Michael Brown] had a dream, because he made rap songs, they may have had cuss words in them. Yeah. He was human. And when we neglect to see that we end up where we are today.

Activists like Yates have also used the claim of humanity to challenge the politics of respectability, a black middle-class ideology that has its origins in the turn-of-the-twentieth century response to black people's loss of civil and political rights following Reconstruction's collapse. The politics of respectability is invested in changing the personal behavior and culture of poor and working-class black people, rather than squarely addressing the structural barriers that keep them locked into a perpetual state of marginality.

This appeal to humanity too has deep—though hidden—roots in the history of the black freedom struggle. The eighteenth-century anti-slavery campaign roused the consciousness of nations by pleading to those who kept them and profited from their bondage, "Am I Not a Man and a Brother?" The agitation of the anti-lynching campaigns of the first half of the twentieth century highlighted the inhumanness of mob violence against black people. Striking garbage workers fighting for a living wage in Memphis in 1968 carried with them placards proclaiming, "I am a Man." But with the successful passage of major civil rights legislation—specifically the 1964 Civil Rights Act, 1965 Voting Rights Act, and the 1968 Fair Housing Act—and the expansion of these laws in subsequent decades, the language of civil rights came to dominate both the ideas and the strategies of leaders and organizations concerned with racial inequality.

With Black Lives Matter, we now have a revival of these historical roots. Its recognition that all black lives deserve humanity, regardless of their gender, class, or sexual orientation, has breathed new life into the legacy of the black freedom struggle. Today's new—and much larger—movement is also articulating the national struggle for racial justice as a broader one for human rights.

In 1951, the "We Charge Genocide" campaign—which included William Patterson, Paul Robeson, W.E.B. Du Bois, Claudia Jones, and family members of victims of racial violence such as Josephine Grayson and Rosalie McGee—petitioned the United Nations to examine human rights abuses against black Americans. The petitioners sought to frame their claims—that African Americans were being persecuted, denied the right to vote, and "pauperized" because of their race—as a question of both black humanity and as a human rights issue: "[A]bove all we protest this genocide as human beings whose very humanity is denied and mocked."

The horrific evidence compiled for the petition, culled from stories in black newspapers and accounts collected by civil rights and labor organizations from 1945 to 1951, is eerily similar to the accounts we hear today. We may be more familiar with the evidence that petitioners document in the Jim Crow South, but the incidents recorded outside it are especially revealing. In many pockets of the urban North, the policing of black migrants was merely a parallel to the Jim Crow violence that terrorized them in the South.

For instance, in February 1946 in Freeport, Long Island, a policeman shot and killed two unarmed black men, wounded a third, and arrested a fourth for "disorderly conduct." The men had objected to being denied service in a café. The Freeport police, in a move that resembles the police's response to protesters in

Ferguson, "threw a cordon around the bus terminal and stationed men with tommy guns and tear gas there, saying that they wanted to 'prevent a possible uprising of local Negroes.'"

Three months later in Baltimore, police shot and killed Wilbur Bundley. "Nine witnesses stated that he was shot in the back while running," the petition reports. In July, Lucy Gordy James, a member of a prominent family of "Negro business people in Detroit," was "beaten severely" by three police officers. "She sued the officers for $10,000 damages, charging illegal arrest, assault, and maltreatment." And in 1951 in Philadelphia, "forty police officers killed an unarmed 21-year-old Negro youth, Joseph Austin Conway, allegedly being sought for questioning in a robbery. He died in a hail of bullets while seeking to draw fire away from his family and neighbors." This catalogue of disaster—to quote James Baldwin—is documented in over 200 pages.

In the 1950s, Malcolm X and Martin Luther King also used the language of human rights to internationalize the issue of racial inequality in the United States. During his travels abroad, Malcolm X enlisted the assistance of heads of states in Africa and the Middle East to condemn the United States for their treatment of black Americans. He discovered that by framing the mistreatment of black Americans as an international human rights issue instead of a national civil rights one, "those grievances can then be brought into the United Nations and be discussed by people all over the world." For him, as long as the discussion was centered on civil rights, "your only allies can be the people in the next community, many of whom are responsible for your grievance." Malcolm X wanted "to come up with a program that would make our grievances international and make the world see that our problem was no longer a Negro problem or an American problem but a human problem."

In framing racial discrimination in human rights terms, the Black Lives Matter movement is today picking up the baton of civil rights activists before them. The parents of Trayvon Martin and Jordan Davis have raised the issue of discriminatory policing with members of the UN Committee on the Elimination of All Forms of

Racial Discrimination in Geneva. The parents of Mike Brown along with representatives of organizations in Ferguson and Chicago traveled to Geneva to share information about their cases with the UN Committee Against Torture in November 2014. Brown's parents submitted a statement to the Committee that read in part, "The killing of Mike Brown and the abandonment of his body in the middle of a neighborhood street is but an example of the utter lack of regard for, and indeed dehumanization of, black lives by law enforcement personnel." Following its examination of the United States, the Committee Against Torture recommended that it undertake independent and prompt investigations into allegations of police brutality and expressed concerns about racial profiling and the "growing militarization of policing activities." After it reviewed the human rights record of the United States this May, a review procedure of the UN Human Rights Council recommended strengthening legislation to combat racial discrimination and addressing excessive use of force by the police.

When Anthony Scott saw the video of his brother Walter Scott being shot as he fled a North Charleston police officer, he remarked, "I thought that my brother was gunned down like an animal." It is a curious thing for black people in the twenty-first century to once again have to claim their humanity. We live in a society where people are more likely to be convicted of animal cruelty than police officers are likely to be charged for the murder of unarmed black, brown, and poor people. But with the Black Lives Matter movement, black America's struggle for human rights is once again gaining strength. Hopefully this time, we can win the more than century-long campaign that has demanded of our nation simply to see us as human.

> "*The 'evidence' supporting the claim that Black Lives Matter is a violent movement largely involves inaccurate anecdotes. The stories are frequently cherry-picked and dismiss important details that drastically change the narrative.*"

Comparing BLM to White Supremacists Is Ludicrous and Dangerous

Melanie Schmitz

In the following viewpoint, Melanie Schmitz rails against the implication made by the right-wing and alt-right media that Black Lives Matter is as radical and dangerous as white supremacist groups. Such comparisons have arisen because white supremacy has returned to visibility during the Trump administration. Schmitz cites statistics about violence and murder that she believes proves the point that there is no comparison. She also provides evidence that the right-wing media seeks to twist the truth to place Black Lives Matter on the same plane as those that preach white supremacy. Schmitz is Associate Editor at ThinkProgress.

"There is no comparison between white supremacists and Black Lives Matter," by Melanie Schmitz, ThinkProgress, August 16, 2017. This article was created by ThinkProgress (www.thinkprogress.org). Reprinted by permission.

As you read, consider the following questions:

1. What percent of all extremist killings in the United States are perpetrated by white supremacists?
2. Why does the author blame right-wing media outlets for the negative perception of Black Lives Matter?
3. Which conservative cable network does the author cite as giving validity to comparisons between Black Lives Matter and white supremacists?

In response to a white supremacist and neo-Nazi rally in Charlottesville, Virginia that left three people dead, much of the conservative media has unified behind a single talking point: What about Black Lives Matter?

On Fox & Friends, co-host Pete Hegseth claimed that "violent aspects of Black Lives Matter ought be called out" during a segment of the show's Sunday edition. Across social media, people equated the group with violent white supremacist factions, insisting that both sides were to blame. On Wednesday, right-wing filmmaker Dinesh D'Souza claimed outright that "alt-left terrorist[s]" associated with Black Lives Matter were "just as dangerous–if not more–than any white nationalist."

President Trump himself echoed the point. "Many sides," he claimed, were to blame for the bloodshed. "[It's been] going on for a long time in our country," he said on Saturday, after news broke that one counter-protester—a 32-year-old woman named Heather Heyer—had been struck and killed when an alleged white supremacist rammed his car into the crowd.

In a press conference intended to address infrastructure on Tuesday, Trump took the narrative one step further: the "alt-left" and counter-protesters (of which Heyer was a part) were to blame for the violence over the weekend. "I think there's blame on both sides," he said. "I have no doubt about it."

Although Trump avoided singling out Black Lives Matter directly, it was clear that Trump was lumping civil rights activists with white nationalists.

Claims that Black Lives Matter presents a violent threat, however, began long before Saturday's rally.

"[In the wake of the Ferguson, Missouri protests] I watched the birth of what is one of the most dangerous and disruptive and divisive leftist approach[es] to tearing down this country," said radio host and Fox News contributor David Webb in July 2016, shortly after a black gunman opened fire on a crowd of police officers in Dallas, Texas, killing five. "A collusion between groups that frankly are anti-American. That's what Black Lives Matter is. You can call it anything else you want."

The gunman was not associated with the Black Lives Matter movement, but that detail mattered little to those looking for a reason to criticize the group and associate it with mass violence.

In July, conservative commentator and NRA spokeswoman Dana Loesch again cast Black Lives Matter as a violent threat, telling Fox News host Tucker Carlson that the group was responsible for any clashes stemming from the protests breaking out across the country. "They've turned to fostering more division instead of solving it," she said.

Those who know the Black Lives Matter movement well, though, vehemently disagree that the group engages in or supports violence.

"In no uncertain terms do I think these [two sides] should be considered equal," said Charles H.F. Davis III, Ph.D, an assistant professor at the Rossier School of Education at the University of Southern California. "People often mischaracterize or misunderstand the context in which the Black Lives Matter movement is taking place—all of it is in response to white terrorism."

More importantly, many people on the ground at rallies who claim black activists are perpetuating violence are only telling half of the story. "Defending oneself is not the same [as what white supremacists in Charlottesville did]," he said.

Manipulating the Narrative

The "evidence" supporting the claim that Black Lives Matter is a violent movement largely involves inaccurate anecdotes. The stories are frequently cherry-picked and dismiss important details that drastically change the narrative.

In the case of the Dallas gunman, Micah Xavier Johnson, authorities said that he had been laughing and singing during the attack and had stated at one point that he "wanted to kill white people, especially white officers"—a phrase that right-wing outlets and anti-black groups quickly picked up on.

Johnson was never actually associated with the Black Lives Matter movement. On Facebook, he had reportedly liked the New Black Panther Party and the African American Defense League, which was founded by Mauricelm-lei Millere, a man known for "calling for violence against police specifically, on a regular basis," Oren Segal of the Anti-Defamation League's Center on Extremism told The New York Times. Local activists said Johnson was not affiliated with any BLM group. Nonetheless, Black Lives Matter leaders quickly issued a response, calling "for an end to violence, not an escalation of it" in a statement after the attack.

The condemnation of Black Lives Matter came anyway. "Clearly the rhetoric of Black Lives Matter encouraged the sniper that shot Dallas police officers," Republican state Rep. Bill Zedler tweeted. On The O'Reilly Factor, Rep. Sean Duffy (R-WI) blasted the group, pinning the blame on President Obama for not condemning it more aggressively. Larry Klayman, a lawyer with radical views on race and government, sued Black Lives Matter for spreading "anti-white" hatred and for supposedly starting a "race war" that culminated in the deaths of the five slain Dallas officers.

The Raw Data

White supremacists are much more likely to commit violent crimes than other sub-groups or classifications of domestic extremism. According to the Anti-Defamation League (ADL), in 2015, white supremacists accounted for 38 percent of all extremist killings, followed closely by Islamist, anti-government, and anti-abortion extremists. Left-wing extremism accounted for around 1 percent of all killings; so-called "black extremism" did not register.

"Typically, white supremacists make up the vast majority of non-ideological perpetrators, as white supremacists engage in a large amount of gang-related and traditional criminal violent activity in addition to their hate- or ideologically-motivated violence," the ADL reported, explaining the numbers. Those groups were often also visibly associated with white supremacist groups—tattoos and insignia on their clothing during the crime often identified them straight off the bat.

By comparison, the number of violent crimes committed by those aligned with civil rights activism is virtually non-existent. Right-wing platforms have attempted to tie black violence in large cities like Chicago to Black Lives Matter, for instance—but it's difficult, if not impossible, to say whether any of those crimes were tied to people aligned with the movement.

In historical terms, white supremacist and neo-Nazi violence also largely overshadows any alleged acts committed by other groups—something Black Lives Matter co-founder Patrisse Cullors is quick to point out.

"This country is rich with an ugly past characterized by genocide, slavery and rooted in white supremacist values to its core," Cullors said, in a statement to ThinkProgress. "[The United States] must come to terms with its past. …[It] must deal with the white supremacy and racism that permeates every institution, the economy, the dominant national culture."

Ultimately, Cullors argues, Trump is empowering white supremacists, making groups like Black Lives Matter even more essential.

"We know that this entire administration, this entire country and its elite political leadership are those very same torch carriers with or without white caps," Cullors said. "As [the president] condones white supremacy, he facilitates a state for white supremacies to continue to terrorize communities of color… especially Black communities."

"A Response to Violence"

Black Lives Matter's biggest voices can claim something the white supremacist movement cannot: They've made an actual effort to denounce racially-charged violence.

In a statement following an attack by a black gunman in Baton Rouge, Louisiana last July that left three police officers dead, prominent Black Lives Matter activist DeRay Mckesson reiterated that "the movement began as a response to violence, it was a call to end violence, and that call to end violence was true two years ago, was true 10 days ago, and is true today."

Here, Davis believes that Black Lives Matter is on the right path. "Changing narrative control is incredibly important," he said. He argued there's something to be said for a widespread denunciation of violence in any form. But, he argues, there are limits to this approach.

"Black Lives Matter has already taken steps to articulate a cohesive message," he said. "What we don't want to have happen, [what] we're not here to respond to is [every violent act]. It's a distraction."

> *"Police are violent agents of the state. They carry weapons, enforce laws that place our communities in danger and use excessive force in order to subdue and 'protect.' Often, the people protesting are the same people who are at most risk for being violated by the police."*

Nonviolent Protest Is a Privilege Not Afforded to All

Nisa Dang

In the following viewpoint, Nisa Dang offers a defense of violence and Black Lives Matter. In reaction to protests that erupted when the University of California-Berkeley invited white nationalist Milo Yiannopoulos to speak to students, the author argues that no protest should be nonviolent. The very police presence on campuses where violent protests against hate speech have unfolded create an atmosphere that leads to violence. The author also seeks to make the point that such invitations alone—those of right-wing provocateurs who espouse violence against blacks and other minorities, are more than deserving of a violent reaction. Dang is a political strategist with a background in social justice, policy research, and issue-based advocacy.

"Check your privilege when speaking of protests," by Nisa Dang, The Daily Californian, February 7, 2017. Reprinted by permission.

As you read, consider the following questions:

1. What reasoning does the author give for her contention that no protest is nonviolent?

2. What white nationalist spurred a violent reaction from protesters when he was invited to speak at the University of California-Berkeley?

3. Why does the author believe there can be no reasonable dialogue with a neo-Nazi?

In light of recent events, there has been a resurgence of the belief that in order for a protest to be effective, it must also be nonviolent. This belief especially plagues liberals, who are talented in drafting long Facebook posts about how they are down with the cause, but not really because windows were broken and some white nationalists got their asses beat. Here's looking at you, Berkeley.

I'm here to explain to this particular segment of the "jolted from a coma, but went back to bed" crowd that they are wrong. Listen closely, because if I have to hear this flawed, problematic and deeply cowardly line of reasoning the next time some people invite a violent fascist-endorsing hate monger to UC Berkeley, we're fighting.

To those campus personalities who made their bread, butter and following by campaigning for ASUC offices and who now feel the need to misinform their constituents by using their glorified platforms, I have news for you. You have a lot to learn about protesting and how it works.

First, no protest is nonviolent. You are laboring under the assumption that protesters are coming into a peaceful atmosphere and disrupting it through chanting, song and broken windows. This, of course, is a misrepresentation of our society and its treatment of the marginalized. For the sake of this brief explanation, let's f--- the broken windows and get straight to the reason so many students were compelled to protest Milo Yiannopoulos' event. From the outset, marginalized student communities have been extremely vocal about the violent impact of Yiannopoulos' appearances and his consistent abuse of platforms. He was banned from Twitter for "participating in or inciting targeted abuse of individuals." He outed a trans woman during an appearance at UW Milwaukee, an act that placed this individual's life in danger. And he had plans to name undocumented students in our community as part of his appearance at UC Berkeley, an act that, in the time of Donald Trump, places our classmates at an even greater risk of being attacked. This is violence. If I know that you are planning to attack me, I'll do all I can to throw the first punch.

Let's move on and discuss the atmospheres created during protests, when police are invited to monitor citizens practicing their right to assembly. I don't care what Breitbart article or liberal bull---- listicle you've read, or what your experiences in white suburbia might have taught you—police are violent agents of the state. They carry weapons, enforce laws that place our communities in danger and use excessive force in order to subdue and "protect." Often, the people protesting are the same people who are at most risk for being violated by the police. Thus, the presence of police officers in riot gear—armed with less-than-lethal weapons they are more than happy to use on protesters—creates an atmosphere that perpetuates violence on community members.

Look—no one actually wants to protest. The decision arose in the face of the fact that the student body was not taken seriously when it said, repeatedly, a million times over, that inviting Yiannopoulos to campus was probably a bad idea. From where I was standing, there was no actual dialogue about why Yiannopoulos should be invited to campus, despite his violent actions and despite the fact that—as evidenced by recent events— most of the student body didn't want him there. (Besides, can you really have meaningful dialogue with people who, at their core, want to eliminate you? The answer is no.) And if Berkeley College Republicans really wanted him—and it really did—well, he came. But for every action, there is a reaction. Just as you all claim that he should be allowed a platform on campus (under the guise of weird misrepresentation of plurality of ideas or whatever), students are allowed to protest him.

To Milo: I'm sorry that you were too scared to stand your ground during a routine Berkeley protest. Hopefully, you'll think twice now about recruiting at my alma mater, where hate speech may be allowed a platform by the administration but will never be tolerated by the student body. Here's a big f---- you from the descendants of people who survived genocides by killing Nazis and people just like them.

To people with platforms who decide when a protest should and should not be violent: You speak from a place of immense privilege. As I recently wrote in a tirade against this brand of idiocy, asking people to maintain peaceful dialogue with those who legitimately do not think their lives matter is a violent act. Putting #LoveTrumpsHate at the end of a post is a privilege that many of you take advantage of, especially when there are those of us who know that our grandparents and parents survived hate only through the grace of violent action. No offense.

Periodical and Internet Sources Bibliography

The following articles have been selected to supplement the diverse views presented in this chapter.

Melinda Anderson "The other student activists," *The Atlantic*, November 23, 2015. https://www.theatlantic.com/education/archive/2015/11/student-activism-history-injustice/417129/

Aware-LA "Statement of solidarity with student organizers on college campuses," December 8, 2015. https://www.awarela.org/news/2017/3/12/statement-of-solidarity-with-student-organizers-on-college-campuses

Alec Brust "Brust: Black Lives Matter needs to establish a new means of protest to succeed," The Rocky Mountain Collegian, July 13, 2017.

Jessica Chasmar "Black Lives Matter protesters berate white students studying at Dartmouth library," *Washington Times*, November 16, 2015. https://www.washingtontimes.com/news/2015/nov/16/black-lives-matter-protesters-berate-white-student/

Aviva Chomsky "Student protest, the Black Lives Matter movement and the rise of the corporate university," Truth-out, May 22, 2016. http://www.truth-out.org/news/item/36135-student-protest-the-black-lives-matter-movement-and-the-rise-of-the-corporate-university

Henry "The University of Chicago is made of safe spaces," Crooked Timber, August 27, 2016. http://crookedtimber.org/2016/08/27/the-university-of-chicago-is-nothing-more-and-nothing-less-than-a-complex-of-safe-spaces/

Corey Mitchell "Programs aim to smooth student-police relations," Education Week, May 19, 2015. https://www.edweek.org/ew/articles/2015/05/20/program-aims-to-smooth-student-police-relations.html

Robby Soave "Black Lives Matter shut down the ACLU's campus free speech event because 'liberalism is white supremacy,'" Reason.com, October 4, 2017. http://reason.com/blog/2017/10/04/black-lives-matter-students-shut-down-th

Telesur "50 years later: The Watts uprising and Ferguson," August 11, 2015. https://www.telesurtv.net/english/news/50-Years-Later-The-Watts-Uprising-and-Ferguson-20150811-0037.html

Ada Harvey Wingfield "Dear CEOs: Those campus racism protests may be coming to your office," *Fortune*, March 6, 2016. http://fortune.com/2016/03/06/protests-racism-corporations/

CHAPTER 4

Are African Americans Really Treated Worse by Law Enforcement?

Chapter Preface

Though side issues are sometimes explored, the very viability of Black Lives Matter rests upon its claim that law enforcement, as a whole, believes that the lives of African Americans are more disposable than those of whites. The viewpoints in this chapter confront that contention.

Like most of those on all sides of the issues relating to the Black Lives Matter organization, the authors of the following viewpoints generally do not hold extremist opinions. They neither claim that no police officers discriminate in their hearts and minds against black citizens, nor that all of them do. Whether one can contend that the police mistreat African Americans in comparison to whites is based on the percentage that do, as well as the establishment of policies in police departments that train tolerance and ensure punishment for any officer that does not practice equal treatment under the law.

It cannot be argued that significant steps have been taken by law enforcement departments across the United States to shorten the gap between officers and the black communities they police. Dashboard cameras have been placed on police cars and body cameras on police uniforms to reveal the truth about confrontations. Sensitivity training and greater awareness of issues pertinent to inner city residents have led to greater understanding and hope for the future. This chapter will explore advances in relations between the two sides, including the weeding out of "bad apples" in police departments that have proven themselves unworthy of their badges.

But this chapter also touches upon court rulings that have absolved police officers of responsibility for shootings of unarmed blacks and how those decisions have negatively affected the perception of many African Americans about fairness in the country in which they live. Rulings in favor of police holding smoking guns have resulted in greater anger of African Americans who already feel like they are targeted unfairly.

> "*Black people make up only 13% of the US population—yet 24% of all the people killed by the police are black. Furthermore, 32% of these black victims were unarmed when they were killed. That's twice the number of unarmed white people to die at the hands of the police.*"

Statistics on Shootings Speak for Themselves

Alem Tedeneke

In the following viewpoint, Alem Tedeneke utilizes statistics to argue that African Americans are disproportionately mistreated by the police. The numbers he studied indicate that Black Lives Matter is justified in its assertion that police shootings are sometimes racially motivated. Tedeneke contends that African-Americans are treated differently than their white counterparts under similar or identical circumstances during confrontations with law enforcement. Also significant is the statistical proof that Americans are more than a hundred times more likely to be killed by police than citizens of other democratic nations around the world. Tedeneke is Media Manager for World Economic Forum USA.

"The Black Lives Matter movement explained," by Alem Tedeneke, World Economic Forum, August 11, 2016. Reprinted by permission.

As you read, consider the following questions:

1. What California activist gave birth to the Black Lives Matter movement through her use of a hashtag?
2. Why does the author claim that some statistics about police shootings in the United States are misleading?
3. What happened to the number of annual police shootings during the Barack Obama administration?

F ollowing high-profile police killings of black men in Baton Rouge and Minneapolis, fatal attacks on officers by anti-police gunmen—and more recently protests in North Carolina after the police shooting of Keith Scott, a black man—the United States is being forced to confront its deep-rooted problems with race and inequality.

A strong narrative is emerging from these tragedies of racially motivated targeting of black Americans by the police force. It is backed up by a new report on the city of Baltimore by the Department of Justice, which has found that black residents of low-income neighbourhoods are more likely to be stopped and searched by police officers, even if white residents are statistically more likely to be caught carrying guns and drugs.

In the background, a campaign called Black Lives Matter celebrated its third anniversary. The movement, perhaps best known by its hashtag #BlackLivesMatter, grew in protest against police killings of black people in the United States. It has now crossed the Atlantic, with events and rallies held in the United Kingdom.

What Is Black Lives Matter?

The movement was born in 2013, after the man who shot and killed an unarmed black teenager, Trayvon Martin, was cleared of his murder. A Californian activist, Alicia Garza, responded to the jury's decision on Facebook with a post that ended: "Black people. I love you. I love us. Our lives matter." The hashtag was born, and continued to grow in prominence with each new incident and protest.

The formal organization that sprung from the protests started with the goal of highlighting the disproportionate number of incidences in which a police officer killed a member of the black community. But it soon gained international recognition, after the death of Michael Brown in Missouri a year later.

Black Lives Matter now describes itself as a "chapter-based national organization working for the validity of black life." It has developed to include the issues of black women and LGBT communities, undocumented black people and black people with disabilities.

Misleading Numbers

According to this article in the *Washington Post*, 1,502 people have been shot and killed by on-duty police officers since the beginning of 2015. A cursory glance at the numbers reveals nothing to indicate racial bias: 732 of the victims were white and 381 were black (382 were of another race).

In fact, on the surface, these figures suggest it's more likely for a white person to be shot by a police officer than a black person. But proportionally speaking, this isn't the case.

Almost half of the victims of police shootings in the US are white, but then, white people make up 62% of the American population. Black people, on the other hand, make up only 13% of the US population—yet 24% of all the people killed by the police are black.

Furthermore, 32% of these black victims were unarmed when they were killed. That's twice the number of unarmed white people to die at the hands of the police.

After adjusting for population percentage, this is the picture: black Americans are two and a half times more likely than white Americans to be shot and killed by police officers.

However, we have to count for distortion of the data, for various reasons. Firstly, it is collected through the voluntary collaboration of police departments with the Federal Bureau of Investigation, so not the full picture. Also, police departments don't always identify a shooting if an officer has been involved. Additionally, police-involved shootings that are under investigation are only counted once the investigation has concluded, so many recent incidents are not being counted.

Don't Other Lives Matter Too?

The slogan "Black Lives Matter", created as a riposte to the institutional racism that lingers on inside the American justice system, has met with its own controversy. Objectors have taken it to mean "black lives matter more". The All Lives Matter campaign, for instance, is one among several groups that have sprung up to argue that every human life, not just those of black people, should be given equal consideration.

The Police Response

In the wake of the mass shooting of five police officers in Dallas in July, a new campaign has taken root. Blue Lives Matter, a national organization made up of police officers and their supporters, places the blame for what they see as a "war on cops" squarely at the feet of the BLM movement and the Obama administration.

But while the data tells a more positive story—that the average number of police officers intentionally killed each year has in fact fallen to its lowest level during Barack Obama's presidency—hate crime is still a daily reality in the US, and many feel that state-wide policies to curb it should be extended beyond the black community to include the police themselves. "Police officers are a minority group, too," former police officer Randy Sutton, a spokesperson for the Blue Lives Matter campaign has been quoted as saying.

Back in Dallas, Chief of Police David Brown has been praised for his efforts to increase transparency and community-friendly policing. He has been credited with a reduction in police-related shootings and fewer complaints about the use of force by police officers.

What's Campaign Zero?

In 2015, the Black Lives Matter movement launched Campaign Zero, a group lobbying for changes to policies and laws on federal, state and local levels.

"We must end police violence so we can live and feel safe in this country," the group writes on the Vision Zero website. "We can live in a world where the police don't kill people—by limiting police interventions, improving community interactions and ensuring accountability."

What Next for Black Lives Matter?

So far, the media has focused on the campaign's events and protests on the street, but Black Lives Matter has also been involved in campaigning to change legislation.

As recently as August this year, the movement released more than 40 policy recommendations, including the demilitarization of law enforcement, reparation laws, the unionization of unregulated industries and the decriminalization of drugs.

Its efforts prior to that have had some success. One example is the creation of a "civilian oversight board" in St Louis City, which reviews and investigates citizens' complaints and allegations of misconduct against the police.

Building on the legacy of the civil rights and LGBT movements, Black Lives Matter has created a new mechanism for confronting racial inequality. The movement also draws on feminist theories of intersectionality, which call for a unified response to issues of race, class, gender, sexuality and nationality.

| "*Video evidence remains susceptible to significant viewer bias.*"

Video Evidence Is Subject to Interpretation

Roseanna Sommers

In following excerpted viewpoint, Roseanna Sommers argues that both white and black Americans support a law that mandates cameras worn by cops to record video of all confrontations. Though cameras have not caught every nuanced movement of interactions in highly publicized shootings of unarmed blacks, they have generally provided enough evidence for those events to be judged properly and effectively. Still, biased interpretation of such footage has resulted in the injustice of officers going unpunished after video evidence seemed to show their guilt. Sommers is a Yale Law School, JD candidate and Yale University Department of Psychology, PhD candidate.

As you read, consider the following questions:

1. Whose murder prompted Barack Obama to call for body cameras on police officers?
2. Approximately what percent of the American public believe placing body cameras on police officers is a good idea?
3. How much more likely were Democrats to support body cameras on cops than Republicans when polled?

In December 2014, President Obama announced the Body Worn Camera Partnership Program, a new initiative to purchase fifty thousand body cameras for use by police officers across the country. The proposal was a response to the fatal police shooting of Michael Brown, an unarmed African American teenager. Brown's death in Ferguson, Missouri, at the hands of Darren Wilson, a Caucasian police officer, sparked weeks of protests decrying police misconduct and racial profiling. The disputed circumstances surrounding Brown's death polarized the nation.[3] A poll administered in Ferguson three months after the shooting found that 71% of Caucasian respondents believed that Wilson was seriously injured before he shot Brown, whereas only 9% of African American respondents agreed. A nationwide poll found that Democrats were over three times more likely than Republicans to say that Wilson was at fault and deserved punishment.

A grand jury decision not to indict Wilson sparked further protests and further polarization. A Washington Post poll conducted after the non-indictment found that nearly 60% of Caucasian respondents approved of the grand jury's decision not to indict Wilson, whereas fewer than 10% of African American respondents approved. Additionally, more than 75% of conservative Republicans approved of the decision, compared to 24% of liberal Democrats. Overall, 48% of the respondents approved of the decision and 45% disapproved.

Many commentators lamented that if only the incident had been captured on camera, we could have known what happened and could have avoided the wrenching societal conflict over the shooting. A writer for *Time* magazine observed, "To many, a camera on Wilson's uniform would have ended the uncertainty and potentially avoided the subsequent tumult that engulfed the St. Louis suburb."

As the country grappled with how to move forward, the months following Brown's death brought a steady drumbeat of high-profile police killings of African American citizens. In July, Staten Island resident Eric Garner was killed by New York Police Department

(NYPD) officer Daniel Pantaleo, who sought to arrest Garner for allegedly selling untaxed cigarettes. A video recorded by a bystander showed that Pantaleo put Garner in a chokehold, a maneuver banned by the NYPD, and ignored repeated pleas from Garner that he was unable to breathe. In November, twelve-year-old Tamir Rice was shot by Cleveland police officers who mistook the boy's pellet gun for a real firearm. Surveillance videos captured the shooting as well as the officers' failure to administer timely first aid to the boy, who died the following day. In April 2015, Walter Scott was shot eight times in the back while fleeing from officer Michael Slager of the North Charleston Police Department, who had pulled Scott over for a broken taillight. Slager initially claimed that he had feared for his life, but an amateur video later surfaced showing that Scott was running away when Slager fired.

As the list of African American men and boys killed by police grows steadily longer, fueling the Black Lives Matter protest movement, advocates for reform have enthusiastically embraced the idea of putting cameras on police officers. Reformers plainly expect that more video footage will lead to more indictments against officers who use excessive force. Indeed, advocates calling for all state and local police to be required to wear cameras have seen fit to name their proposal the "Mike Brown Law."

It was perhaps natural for the White House, in the wake of Brown's death, to turn to body cameras as a solution. In a policy realm with few areas of agreement, body cameras are widely popular. A Pew Research Center poll conducted in December 2014 found that 87% of respondents thought body cameras were a good idea. The support was bipartisan: 79% of Republicans, 90% of Democrats, and 88% of Independents favor the reform. The numbers are similarly high among African American (90%), Hispanic (89%), and Caucasian (85%) respondents.[21] Notably, these figures come from a survey conducted in the days following the Staten Island grand jury's decision not to indict Daniel Pantaleo in Eric Garner's death, even though the episode was captured on video. Following the non-indictment, Garner's father told reporters that the White House's initiative was "[t]hrowing money away. Video didn't matter here." But even after such a high-profile instance of video footage failing to secure an indictment, support for the body camera reform remained high. A poll conducted five months after Pantaleo's non-indictment found that 93% of Caucasian respondents and 93% of African American respondents favor putting video cameras on police officers.

To those who feel that police officers too often get away with murder, body cameras promise to collect the evidence needed to hold police officers accountable. To those who feel that civil rights activists have jumped to conclusions too quickly in ambiguous cases, body cameras offer hard facts that could potentially exonerate officers falsely accused of misconduct. Indeed, despite initial resistance from police departments, precincts that have adopted lapel cameras have largely come to embrace them as a much-needed deterrent to frivolous lawsuits. Even the American Civil Liberties Union, normally an opponent of increased government surveillance, sees body cameras as a "win-win."

The current policy debate over body-worn cameras has highlighted numerous advantages and disadvantages of putting cameras on police officers. Many proponents support body cameras because they believe the police will use unnecessary force less often if they know they are being recorded. Indeed, promising results from a pilot program in Rialto, California found that body cameras were associated with a decrease in use of force. In addition, footage from body-worn cameras provides new opportunities for police training and feedback. Moreover, to law enforcement authorities who fear a growing crisis of legitimacy in their communities, body-worn cameras offer transparency and a way to restore public trust in the police. The other side of the ledger, however, contains concerns about how body cameras will affect citizens' privacy; how the footage will be stored and maintained; and under what conditions the public will have access to the evidence.

This Note does not attempt to provide an all-things-considered recommendation about whether body cameras amount to sound

WHICH APPLES ARE WHICH?

You may have read about Michael Hamill, the "hot cop" from Gainesville, Florida, who became famous for his hunky good looks shortly after Hurricane Irma made landfall in the Sunshine State. You may recall that Hamill's fame immediately exposed him as someone who was comfortable making anti-Semitic jokes online, a transgression for which he promptly was suspended.

A few bad apples, say police apologists, exceptions to the rule. Perhaps. But the "apple" excuse becomes more tiresome and inadequate each day.

It's not just the "bad apples" within police departments who cause citizens to lose confidence and trust in their local police. It's not just the cops who engage in discrimination or other forms of misconduct. It's these "good apples," too, the ones who obey the law, and the rules, but who countenance, excuse, justify, or defend the bad behavior of their friends and colleagues. So many "good apples" spend so much time defending the "bad apples" that it becomes hard to tell which apples are which.

In the wake of Hamill's suspension, Law Officer, a digital news site that's popular among law enforcement, published "Three Lessons from the Gainesville 'Hot Cop' Selfie." All of the lessons offered practical advice to police officers on protecting their online activity from exposure—to be cautious about what they post in the first place and to carefully vet their social networks for controversial views. The recommendations are reasonable on their face, but they would have officers believe the real problem with Hamill's post is that we found out about it.

Instead of advising cops on how to hide their anti-Semitic remarks from public view, instead of portraying Hamill's mistake as one of online carelessness, the writer of the piece could and should have held Hamill accountable for his posts and encouraged his network to do the same. Lesson one should have been: If you know someone on the force who holds these views, report them, so that your entire department isn't infected by those views and their potential impact on the people you are sworn to protect and serve.

"How Bad Apples Spoil the Whole Bunch," by Andrew Cohen, The Marshall Project, September 27, 2017.

public policy. Rather, it assesses one salient argument that is frequently made in favor of body cameras: that they will reduce societal conflict and polarization by offering definitive proof of what happened.

Proponents of body cameras often argue that video footage can provide unambiguous records of police-civilian encounters. For instance, when the New Jersey legislature approved a bill requiring local police to be filmed by in-car or body-worn cameras, the sponsor of the bill touted video footage as providing "an unbiased, accurate record [of] what transpired." Video recordings of police interrogations of suspects, for their part, have been hailed as "ready and available as an objective offer of proof." As Philadelphia Police Commissioner Charles Ramsey explained, "Everybody's got their version of a story, but when it's on tape, it's on tape. . . . It is what it is."

But the assumption that video evidence will help resolve disputes over whether misconduct occurred will bear out only if fact finders reviewing the footage can agree on what it shows. If they cannot agree—if, for example, they conform their perceptions of facts to their expectations or preferred outcomes—then cameras may fail to deliver on the promise of definitively resolving polarizing disputes.

This Note examines the potential for fact finders to evaluate even hard video evidence in biased ways while simultaneously becoming more confident that their judgments are unbiased. It argues that, in at least some cases, psychological factors can conspire to produce biased factual findings, even among viewers who are sincerely trying to evaluate the evidence fairly and impartially. In particular, it finds that video evidence remains susceptible to significant viewer bias and simultaneously causes some fact finders—namely those who feel a strong affinity with police officers—to become more certain of their judgments and more resistant to persuasion by others who disagree. It concludes that while presenting fact finders with video footage probably does not exacerbate biased decision-making, we lack evidence that it constitutes an improvement over the status quo.

This Note focuses on how video evidence interacts with cognitive processes that lead well-intentioned people to form opposing views of the same situation. It does not analyze cases where video footage exposes blatant corruption or dishonesty. For instance, it does not examine cases like Walter Scott's shooting by Michael Slager. Slager initially claimed that he discharged his weapon because Scott had taken his Taser and he felt threatened. But video footage captured by a pedestrian shows that at the time Slager fired, Scott was fifteen to twenty feet away and fleeing. And the video shows Slager picking up an object from the ground and dropping it by Scott's body, leading some viewers to conclude that Slager was planting the Taser on Scott to make his account more believable. Commentators noted that this case "deviated greatly" from the familiar "template for controversial police shootings," because once the video surfaced, "there was hardly the typical closing of ranks around Slager" by other police and he was quickly charged with murder.

This Note does not examine such cases, where one party has outright lied about what happened, and video footage debunks the fabricated version of events. Rather, it looks at a far more familiar and ordinary phenomenon: different people forming contradictory interpretations of the same event.

> "*The police use force mainly to protect human life, the use of force against unarmed suspects is rare, and the use of force against black Americans is largely proportional to their share of the violent crime rate.*"

Numbers Tell Terrible Truth About Black Lives Matter

David French

In the following viewpoint, David French is asserts through statistical analysis that criticism of police in America regarding unequal treatment of minorities is unwarranted. French cites significantly higher crime rates among African Americans that he says result in a larger number of confrontations with law enforcement that naturally lead to more fatalities. Though some studies have shown that blacks are more likely than whites to be killed in similar confrontations, French maintains his view that a few bad apples among officers should not spoil the reputations of police departments in general. French is a lawyer and staff writer for the National Review, one of the foremost conservative publications in the United States.

As you read, consider the following questions:

1. A study from what newspaper considered by some as liberal-leaning did the author use to make an argument embraced by conservatives?
2. What is the basis of French's claim that Black Lives Matter is off-base in its basic claim that police are discriminatory?
3. Approximately what percentage of killings at the hands of police in 2015 were of unarmed victims?

Ever since the explosion of the Black Lives Matter movement, Americans have been bombarded with assertions that black men face a unique and dangerous threat—not from members of their own community but from the very law enforcement officers who are sworn to "serve and protect" them. Hashtags such as #DrivingWhileBlack and #WalkingWhileBlack have perpetuated a narrative that black Americans risk being gunned down by police simply because of the color of their skin. Using individual anecdotes of police misconduct and the now-discredited "hands up, don't shoot" rallying cry, Black Lives Matter has built a case that American police are out of control.

The conservative response is clear: While no one believes the police are perfect, on the whole they tend to use force appropriately to protect their own lives and the lives of others. Moreover, racial disparities in the use of force are largely explained by racial disparities in criminality. Different American demographics commit crimes at different rates, so it stands to reason that those who commit more crimes will confront the police more often. Yes, there are rogue officers—and those rogue officers should be prosecuted—but the police are still a force for good in our society.

In response to the allegations of Black Lives Matter activists, the *Washington Post* launched an unprecedented, case-by-case study of police shootings. After a year of research, the data are in, and they confirm the conservative position: The police use force mainly to protect human life, the use of force against unarmed

Violence Against Police

The FBI has released some sobering numbers on violence experienced by law enforcement officers. In 2016, over 57,000 officers were assaulted while on duty and 118 died. That's up 37% from 2015 when 86 officers died in the line of duty.

In total, 66 police officers were murdered last year. Here's the breakdown:

- 17 officers were killed in ambush situations, a macabre byproduct of the Black Lives Matter movement.
- 13 officers who died had responded to disturbance calls.
- 9 officers died as a result of investigating suspicious persons or circumstances.
- 9 officers died as a result of arrest situations.
- 6 officers were killed as a result of tactical situations (barricaded offender, hostage taking, high-risk entry, etc.).
- 5 officers were conducting investigative activities (surveillance, search, interview, etc.).
- 4 officers were fatally injured during traffic pursuits/stops.
- 3 officers were killed in unprovoked attacks.

The average stats for the officers killed are as follows: 40 years old, 13 years service, nearly all male and white. Only four were black and one was Asian/Native Hawaiian/Other Pacific Islander. The majority of officers were wearing body armor at the time.

The Left portrays officers as kill-happy soldiers shooting wildly in all directions. But of those officers murdered, only 14 fired their weapons and 11 attempted to fire. Three of the officers had their weapons stolen. The shooting deaths of 19 cops occurred when they were just five feet or less from the perpetrators.

The remaining 52 deaths were accidental, such as vehicle accidents and being unintentionally hit by motor vehicles.

According to the report, 57,180 officers were assaulted in 2016 and 29%, or 16,535 sustained injuries. In 2015, the number of officers assaulted was 50,212.

"All of these numbers increased from figures reported in 2015, when 45 officers died accidentally and 41 were feloniously killed in the line of duty," the report noted.

"FBI Report: 57,000 Officers Assaulted While on Duty, 66 Killed in 2016," by Trey Sanchez, TruthRevolt.org, October 16, 2017.

suspects is rare, and the use of force against black Americans is largely proportional to their share of the violent crime rate.

According the *Post*, as of December 24, American police had fatally shot 965 people in 2015. (The Guardian, in the midst of its own study, reports a slightly higher number of shootings). 564 of those killed were armed with a gun, 281 were armed with another weapon, and 90 were unarmed. In fully three-quarters of shootings, "police were under attack or defending someone who was."

But what of race? The kinds of shootings that launched the Black Lives Matter movement—white police officers killing unarmed black men—represent "less than 4 percent of fatal police shootings." The Post does its best to hype the racial injustice of this statistic, proclaiming that while "black men make up only 6 percent of the U.S. population, they account for 40 percent of the unarmed men shot to death by police this year." But that claim is misleading on a number of counts.

Crime doesn't break down on neat, proportionate demographic lines. Criminals are overwhelmingly male (police killed very few women this year, but no one argues that law enforcement is sexist), and violent criminals are disproportionately black. In fact, blacks "commit homicide at close to eight times the rate of whites and Hispanics combined." Even worse, "among males between the ages of 14 and 17, the interracial homicide commission gap is nearly tenfold." In 2014, for example, while black Americans constituted only about 13 percent of the population, they represented a majority of the homicide and robbery arrests. 82 percent of all gun deaths in the black community are from homicide. For whites, 77 percent of gun deaths are suicides.

Given these disturbing disparities, no rational person would expect police shootings to precisely track with demographics. Police follow crime, and they tend to operate in high-crime areas. It would be alarming if there were statistically significant racial variations in the use of force even after adjusting for crime rate, but the *Post*'s report doesn't make this distinction. Even the "hugely disproportionate" ratio—"3 in 5"—of blacks and Hispanics shot to death after "exhibiting less threatening behavior" than brandishing a gun isn't out of line with violent-crime rates.

The report does highlight areas where law-enforcement agencies could do better—improved training in handling fleeing or mentally ill suspects could save lives, for example—and while police are generally responsible in the use of force, that doesn't mean that all use of force is lawful. There are individual racist cops, and there are departments that will close ranks behind corrupt colleagues. But the chances of an innocent black man being gunned down by racist cops are vanishingly small. And that is good news indeed.

While I am no fan of social movements built on false narratives, Black Lives Matter did inspire the *Post*'s valuable study—a study that, fairly read, should defuse national tensions. It won't, however. The narrative is too strong, and too many powerful people have too much to gain by ratcheting up racial tensions. So Black Lives Matter will likely roll on, and still more black Americans will be taught to hate and fear law enforcement, fed on a steady diet of lies about their own country. America is a better place than they've been led to believe. Radical racial politics will only make it worse.

> *"If this issue had instead been framed as an increasingly militarized, reactionary police force, support for reform could have come from all across American society. Instead, support is now clearly divided along racial and political lines."*

Police Brutality Cannot Be All About Race

Universal Life Christian Monastery

In the following viewpoint, the Universal Life Christian Monastery gives a straight-forward and seemingly unbiased examination of highly publicized police confrontations with unarmed young black men that gave rise to Black Lives Matter. The author laments the murders of police by black assailants that followed, but cites the killings of unarmed African-Americans at the hands of law enforcement as a catalyst to that violence. The author makes a plea for peace and greater understanding on both sides but also decries the notion put forth by Black Lives Matter that the police are racially motivated in many of its actions. The Universal Life Christian Monastery is a nonprofit, nondenominational religious organization committed to religious freedom and social justice.

"Wave of Violence: Police Brutality and Racial Conflict in America," Universal Life Church Ministries, July 19, 2016. Reprinted by permission.

As you read, consider the following questions:

1. Does the author subscribe to the "bad apples" theory, which states that a number of racist cops are giving the rest a bad name?
2. Can this article be considered biased for or against Black Lives Matter?
3. What general solution to improve police-community relations is put forth here?

America is a country divided in many ways. Politically, we are more polarized than at any time in recent memory. Economically, much of the country's wealth is concentrated in the hands of an elite few. But most glaring is this: despite years of progress on race relations, animosity continues to endure across racial lines. Unfortunately, recent incidents around the country make up the latest chapter in a long history of conflict between white and black America.

The ULC strongly condemns this violence. Our guiding belief is that we are all children of the same universe, and as such we must work together to find a solution to this conflict. Our goal here is to present both sides of the issue and encourage a unified effort in the face of division.

Alton Sterling and Philando Castile

The tragic deaths of Alton Sterling and Philando Castile earlier this month sparked national outrage. Both were black men, gunned down by police in separate shootings within two days of each other. They quickly became the latest martyrs for police reform. Plenty of police shootings occur every year, but these specific cases proved especially provocative because they were caught on camera.

Bystanders were filming as officers confronted Alton Sterling. He was thrown to the ground and surrounded by police, but didn't appear to be fully compliant with police commands. During the struggle, the officers realized Sterling had a gun on him—things escalated rapidly and the encounter ended with Sterling being shot multiple times in the chest.

Philando Castile's girlfriend began Facebook live-streaming in the moments after Castile was shot during a routine traffic stop. According to reports, Castile immediately informed police that he was carrying a gun. He then began to reach for his driver's license. The officers reportedly thought he was going for his gun, and promptly opened fire. The video aftermath shows Castile bleeding out in the passenger seat as his girlfriend offers chilling commentary on the injustice of the shooting. After much contemplation, we've decided to include the video in this post.

Retaliatory Violence

Millions of Americans saw these videos as fresh examples of a glaring injustice—the tendency of police officers to kill black men without good cause. The latest resurgence in public fury was led by the Black Lives Matter (BLM) movement, which organized scores of peaceful protests across the country.

Then, what had been a nonviolent protest in Dallas quickly turned to tragedy—five police officers were killed and a half-dozen others injured after a lone gunman opened fire. The shooter, who had no connection to BLM, appeared to be acting in retaliation to the recent police shootings—stating that he "wanted to kill white officers." Tensions raised even higher, and it seemed as if things could not get any worse. But over this past weekend, it did. Another gunman seeking vengeance against police opened fire, this time in Baton Rouge, killing another three officers. That span of 10 days was the deadliest period for law enforcement in America since 9/11.

This recent spate of violence has triggered criticism of the Black Lives Matter movement.

Black Lives Matter

Black Lives Matter describes itself as "an ideological and political intervention in a world where Black lives are systematically and intentionally targeted for demise". For the past few years BLM has been growing in strength, leading protests all across America in response to police shootings of black men. However, it has also been criticized for being disorganized and lacking clear policy goals.

More of a philosophy than a structured organization, BLM operates without formal leadership or hierarchy. Critics argue that this has inadvertently led to violence. They contend that a lack of guidance has led some to interpret the phrase "Black Lives Matter" as a call-to-arms.

Just as extremists throughout history have used religion as an excuse to commit violent acts, several radical individuals have used the banner of Black Lives Matter to falsely justify violence. Of course, that it far from the original intent of the movement. BLM itself is based on a simple moral ideal—that everyone deserves to be treated equally by the law. So why aren't they?

By the Numbers

The key piece of evidence in favor of police reform is the fact that black people are being killed by police in disproportionate numbers. The *Washington Post* examined these numbers and found that of the 1,502 people shot and killed by police since January of last year, 732 were white, 381 were black, and the remainder were of another race. However, black Americans make up only 13 percent of the population. Adjusting for this, black people in the U.S. are 2.5 times more likely to be shot and killed by police than whites. Even more staggering are the rates at which unarmed black people are killed by police, pictured at right. Obviously, these are profound disparities.

Critics, though, are quick to counter that black Americans also commit a disproportionate amount of crime. A look at FBI crime statistics for the 75 largest counties in America backs up this claim. Although they make up just 15 percent of the population, in these counties black Americans are charged with 45 percent of assaults, 62 percent of robberies, 57 percent of murders. This, too, is a striking imbalance.

Supporters of law enforcement defend police actions in black communities by arguing that since violent crime is much more likely to occur in these areas, police need to be on guard and ready to defend themselves. For them, split-second decisions can be the difference between life and death.

The Problem with Bad Apples

We are heartbroken by the recent shootings of police in Dallas and Baton Rouge. Being a police officer is undoubtedly one of the toughest jobs out there. However, it would be foolish to claim this issue is one-sided. While violence against police can never be defended, we must also acknowledge the troubling police culture which exists in America. It is overly-aggressive, nontransparent, and perpetuates a toxic "Us vs. Them" mentality.

For all the good the police do, there are always a number of police officers that engage in corrupt or violent behavior. To make things worse, police also have a terrible habit of defending one another regardless of circumstance. This phenomenon is often referred to as the "blue wall of silence". Whenever bad behavior does come to light, there are loud calls for police reform. However, time and time again these demands are spurned—the public is ensured that "it's just a few bad apples" causing problems. But this is a terrible analogy. Let us not forget the saying: those few bad apples can easily spoil the whole barrel.

Takeaways

Black Lives Matter has electrified the movement for police reform by decrying racial mistreatment. Sadly, that very idea may prove to be the movement's undoing. The woeful reality is that race remains a divisive subject in America. Because of this, the portrayal of police brutality as a purely racial problem has likely killed any chance of legitimate reform in the near future. If this issue had instead been framed as an increasingly militarized, reactionary police force, support for reform could have come from all across American society. Instead, support is now clearly divided along racial and political lines. As we have seen in Dallas and Baton Rouge, such a dynamic only encourages further hostility and violence.

If there is one thing everyone can agree on, it's this: the violence needs to stop. We need to come together as a nation and focus on unity instead of division. By continuing to attack each other, we will only make things worse. As the late Mahatma Gandhi famously said, "an eye for an eye makes the whole world blind."

> *"The benefits of thorough and unbiased investigations easily outweigh such notions of territorialism. The result will be greater trust in the process and increased legitimacy of the criminal justice system in the eyes of the public."*

Only Independent Investigations Can Create Trust

Walter Katz

In the following viewpoint, Walter Katz tackles one of the most pressing and divisive issues in the scope of police-community relations. Police investigations into shootings of unarmed black men have most often not resulted in convictions. And that has led to frustration, protests, and even retaliation against officers by African Americans seeking justice, though there has been no evidence that such attacks were motivated by Black Lives Matter. The author calls for independent investigations into such incidents, which he believes would legitimize outcomes and create a greater sense of trust in the process. Katz is Deputy Chief of Staff for Public Safety, Office of the Mayor, City of Chicago.

As you read, consider the following questions:

1. What positive consequences could result from independent investigations into police shootings?
2. Which tragic events did the author cite in making his argument that investigations should be taken out of police hands?
3. How does the law background of the author bolster the strength of his proposals?

There are few acts committed by local government that draw more controversy than a police department's use of lethal force. Broad cross-sections of the public have lost trust in local law enforcement agencies due to their perception of biased investigations of such deadly-force incidents. This loss of trust can threaten the legitimacy of local law enforcement institutions. Systemic reforms are necessary to regain trust. Generally, the courts are not a vehicle to bring about such reforms absent the active involvement of the Department of Justice. In the current system of shooting investigations, the involved officer's own agency investigates the fatal use of force before turning the case over to the local prosecutor for review. Is there a more effective way to scrutinize the actions of officers in the United States while still protecting their due process rights? In fact, there are models in other countries which are designed to produce bias-free investigations that enhance public trust in, and the legitimacy of, the government. The various states should look to these other systems and create independent agencies to investigate and also, where necessary, to prosecute police-related deaths.

An often-told maxim is that a state is characterized by a "monopoly of the legitimate use of physical force."[1] That may or may not be true, but the "legitimacy of the use of force is central to the modern concept of governance."[2] The traditional point of view of the state's ability to use force is that without such a monopoly, its capacity to enforce the rule of law and protect its citizens is constrained.[3] This perspective is reflected in traditional crime control policies that use deterrent threat and increasing severity of sanctions to gain compliance from potential lawbreakers.[4]

One result of such a traditional crime control model, not just in this country but around the world, is that immigrant communities and ethnic minorities become disproportionate targets.[5] The New York Police Department uses an assertive policing model (which is well known as "broken windows") that targets low-level quality of life transgressions with the goal of deterring more serious crimes.[6] Critics of the strategy argue it unfairly singles out minorities.[7] New York City's Civilian Complaint Review Board (CCRB) found that while African Americans made up 23% of the city's population, they represented 55% of reported victims of alleged misconduct from 2008 to 2013.[8] Hispanics were 29% of the population and 26% of complainants, while whites were 34% of the population but were only 9% of alleged victims of police misconduct.[9] In 2013, 53% of all complaints were for some form of alleged physical force misconduct.[10] Periodically, the distrust that this perceived targeting engenders boils over. Public dissatisfaction with the current relationship between the police and ethnic minority communities was clearly put on display in 2014 in response to several high-profile killings by police of young African Americans in the United States: most prominently the chokehold death of Eric Garner in New York and the fatal shooting of Michael Brown in Ferguson, Missouri.

The Brown and Garner cases embodied not only general distrust between police and minority communities, but also the loss of the public's trust in the investigations and reviews of police-involved deaths.[11] When grand juries declined to file criminal charges in both cases, many members of the public did not trust the outcomes, which they saw as tainted by collusion between the police and local prosecutors.[12] Opinion polls taken after the deaths of Brown and Garner demonstrate that significant cross-sections of the public do not believe that investigations of police-involved deaths are fair and impartial. In one survey, 76% of African

Americans had little confidence in investigations such as the one into Brown's death.[13] In another poll, this one by YouGov, less than half—only 42%—of whites "trust[ed] the justice system to properly investigate" police-involved deaths, while a mere 19% of African Americans had such trust in the existing system.[14]

Whether civilians trust the institutions of justice is central to the concept of procedural justice. That is, where the public trusts the process of the justice system, it will confer legitimacy on those institutions.[15] A significant body of research demonstrates "public perceptions of the fairness of the justice system in the United States are more significant in shaping its legitimacy than perceptions that it is effective."[16]

Where the public has trust, it will sanction law enforcement with legitimacy; and when it does so, it is signaling that the public's moral values of right and wrong are aligned with those of its police agencies. Conversely, legitimacy crumbles when civilians are treated unfairly and the public is left with the conclusion that police agencies are not accountable.[17] The lack of trust is not universal and disagreements over law enforcement too often devolve into vituperative attacks over the character of the police as well as protestors. Such arguments, in turn, "induce disputes" over the appropriate design for accountability mechanisms.[18]

For the most part, the process of investigating police-caused fatalities is opaque to the public. Each lethal use of force by an officer is a homicide and investigators and prosecutors must ask whether it was also a crime. Typically police-involved deaths are subject to a two-track investigation. The first investigation is to determine whether the officer committed a crime. In most large agencies, that investigation is conducted internally by detectives from a homicide squad or by a force investigation team.[19] This team is primarily responsible for gathering evidence, locating witnesses and conducting interviews—including that of the involved officer, who has the right to invoke his or her right to remain silent. Other agencies—especially smaller ones—will often have a larger neighboring department or a state police agency conduct the criminal investigation.[20] Once the investigation is completed, it is forwarded to the local prosecutor who, depending on the jurisdiction, either convenes a grand jury or decides whether to directly file charges against the officer.[21] The second investigation is to determine whether the officer violated department policies or tactics. Here, the officer can be compelled to provide a statement; however, such statements cannot be used against him or her in a criminal proceeding.[22] The focus of this Commentary is on the first-described criminal investigation.

This system of internalized criminal investigations has been criticized for years for its inherent bias. Merrick Bobb, the Executive Director of the Police Assessment Resource Center and one of the most well-known and highly respected advocates for effective police oversight, has argued that bias in shooting investigations appears in many forms. Some investigations are "half-hearted, wherein not all relevant witnesses are interviewed or even attempted to be located, particularly those witnesses who might give testimony unfavorable to the officer."[23] Bobb notes that interviewers of involved officers slant investigations by using "softball, open-ended questions" that allow for narrative responses, fail to challenge factual assertions by the officer, and ask leading questions at opportune moments that likely "signal to the officer what he is supposed to say in order to get off the hook."[24] In other words, in the current investigative system, the involved officer is "not investigated as someone who may have reason to fabricate evidence and lie."[25] When the investigator and the subject of the investigation are connected to the same organization, there is a natural impulse to interpret evidence in a way that supports the conclusion the interpreter would prefer.[26] This bias is not unique to law enforcement; it is also visible in other fields where a close relationship exists and strong bonds are formed, such as financial auditing.[27]

Thus where there is a strong affinity with the subject of investigation, "it may be impossible for professionals to fulfill roles that demand objectivity while simultaneously fulfilling roles that demand partisanship."[28]

Nor are local prosecutors immune from bias. In his critique of the Los Angeles criminal justice system following the Rampart scandal (which included an officer-involved shooting that paralyzed an unarmed man with no prior criminal record who was then initially sentenced to prison for twenty-three years after officers planted a gun on him), Dean Erwin Chemerinsky identified a culture within the district attorney's office that discouraged asking too many questions about potential misconduct and exhibited a pro-police bias.[29] This reflected an "institutional ethic of combat" where gaining convictions was prized over all other qualities.[30] Chemerinsky noted that even where prosecutors were suspicious of misconduct, they were reluctant to confront officers, since the police were "handing them all the evidence needed to get a guilty plea or conviction."[31] Since most prosecutions rely on maintaining the credibility of the police, when the on-duty actions of officers are under investigation, "prosecutors face 'an impossible conflict of interest between their desire to maintain working relationships and their duty to investigate and prosecute police brutality.'"[32] As a result, Professor John Jacobi argues, prosecutions for on-duty conduct are a rarity: "civilian distrust can be traced" to the perception of "a cycle of impunity, by which the reluctance of local government to prosecute bad cops empowers future misconduct and drives communities to regard the police as adversaries instead of protectors."[33]

The courts present one possible solution to the problem of biased investigations and rare prosecutions. Limited resources, as well as judicial precedent, however, have made courts an unreliable solution. Federal law prohibits state or local law enforcement officials from "engag[ing] in a pattern or practice of conduct" that deprives persons of rights "protected by the Constitution or laws of the United States."[34] The passage of what is commonly known as the "Law Enforcement Misconduct Statute" was partly in reaction to findings by the Christopher Commission in Los Angeles that the LAPD had exercised "lax supervision" and conducted "inadequate investigation[s]" of potential misconduct.[35] The

Department of Justice (DOJ) is empowered to seek injunctive relief to end the misconduct and force reforms of "policies and procedures that resulted in or allowed the misconduct."[36] The DOJ has recently sought either injunctive relief against or a pre-litigation settlement against a number of police departments in places such as Albuquerque and New Orleans after high-profile shootings.[37] Yet there are approximately 18,000 local agencies in the United States[38] and, until the summer of 2014, no one outside of eastern Missouri had likely ever heard of Ferguson. The DOJ, however, initiates only about three pattern-and-practice investigations a year.39 When a police department has not caught the attention of the DOJ, which often adopts a "worst-first" strategy that prioritizes large agencies, the remedies are sparse.[40]

Litigants have not been successful in bringing claims pursuant to 42 U.S.C. § 1983 that allege police agencies are inadequately investigating shootings. Municipal liability attaches only when the municipality has an official policy or custom that causes an unconstitutional deprivation of the plaintiff's rights.[41] The linkage between inadequate investigations and a policy or custom has proven difficult to establish. In Lee v. City of Richmond,[42] the U.S. District Court for the Eastern District of Virginia ruled that an inadequate investigation claim requires the same showing as a "failure to train" allegation.[43] That is, the inadequacy must have been plainly obvious to city policymakers who were, nevertheless, "deliberately indifferent to the need."[44] The U.S. Court of Appeals for the Seventh Circuit reached a similar conclusion, holding that a plaintiff could not rely on an Illinois grand jury finding that not one of the 783 excessive force complaints made against a sheriff's department over a five-year period resulted in an indictment to support a claim that the sheriff did not in practice enforce policies against excessive use of force.[45]

Private plaintiffs seeking injunctive relief are also unlikely to have success. The Supreme Court has shown great reluctance to using private party injunctive relief to change the investigative practices of police departments.[46] In City of Los Angeles v.

Lyons,[47] the Supreme Court foreclosed the plaintiff from seeking injunctive relief against the LAPD for the use of chokeholds unless he could demonstrate it was likely that its officers would use a chokehold on him again in the future.[48] In a hypothetical suit to enjoin an agency from conducting inadequate police shooting investigations, it would be extremely difficult for a plaintiff to show that he or she would be impacted by inadequate shooting investigations again in the future. Without access to monetary or injunctive relief, impacted communities will need to wait until the Department of Justice, the "sole authority to initiate structural police reform," launches a pattern-and-practice investigation.[49]

Although the courts may not offer a solution to the problem of police and prosecutorial bias in investigating police-involved deaths, state legislatures may. To prevent further erosion of public trust, state legislatures should move the investigation and prosecution of police-involved deaths to independent agencies. A number of countries have built alternative structures to investigate police-caused deaths. These alternative models, adopted in the United Kingdom, Norway, and Canada, are completely independent from the involved agency and, in some cases, even from the local prosecutor.

The Police Ombudsman of Northern Ireland (PONI) was established by the Police (Northern Ireland) Act 1998[50] and opened its doors in 2000.[51] Complaints against the Police Service of Northern Ireland, including allegations of criminal misconduct, are investigated by PONI.[52] By law, PONI "must [also] investigate all cases of death or serious injury."[53] After concluding its investigation, PONI then makes recommendations to the Director of Public Prosecutions who has the discretion whether to file charges.[54]

The Norwegian Parliament created the Norwegian Bureau for the Investigation of Police Affairs in 2004.55 The Norwegian government is explicit that, "[w]ithout adequate control of the [police's] use of [its] power, the right to use force could become a threat to legal protection and democracy."[56] The Norwegian Bureau is independent of the national police force and is administratively attached to the Ministry of Justice.[57] It investigates all allegations of criminal misconduct by officers and all instances where someone dies as a result of the police or prosecuting agency's exercise of their authority and has its own cadre of prosecutors.[58] The Norwegian Bureau exists to safeguard three objectives: "the right for involved persons to be heard," the maintenance of "public confidence in procedures," and the protection of "fundamental rights for citizens and police officers involved."[59]

Surveys conducted in Europe suggest that residents of countries with independent investigation structures have a higher opinion of their criminal justice systems than similar American surveys have shown. While a direct correlation between the public's view of the criminal justice system and independent investigations of police use of force is difficult to measure, researchers surveyed attitudes about justice systems through the European Social Survey in 2010. The survey asked forty-five questions in twenty-eight countries to measure trust in the police and the courts.[60] The survey designers recognized that "[i]f securing normative compliance with the law is to be a key aim of criminal justice policy, then public trust in the system is required. It is equally important that citizens accept the legal institutions as having a legitimate right to exercise authority."[61]

Unfortunately, there is no similar data from prior to the formation of investigation bodies either in the United Kingdom or in Norway against which to compare the 2010 survey, and the ESS asked no questions directly about lethal force investigations. Nevertheless, the results show that even respondents who identified as belonging to groups that experience discrimination in their respective countries had greater confidence in the police than the amount of confidence that ethnic minorities in the United States have in their police. When surveyors asked those in the United Kingdom who were in groups that had experienced discrimination "how often the police make fair, impartial decisions," 69.9% responded "often" or "very often," versus 83.4% of those who had not suffered discrimination.[62] Surveyors also asked whether "[p]olice have the same sense of right or wrong as [the respondent]."

ARE POLICE RESPONSIBLE FOR CHICAGO KILLINGS?

For years there have been rumors and speculation about many of the killings that have occurred in Chicago. Many people in the Melanoid community suspect that police officers are really the ones behind some of these shootings. Chicago has become to go-to deflection talking point for white supremacists (and white supremacist supporters) who use the alleged "Black on Black" violence in Chicago to justify the violence and mistreatment of Melanoid people around the country.

So when we see these recurring reports coming out of Chicago every holiday weekend reporting that a certain "record" number of people were killed or shot over a three day period, and no arrests were made, this raises many red flags with some in the community.

It's not a stretch of the imagination to suspect that law enforcement in Chicago could carry out such corrupt deeds because Chicago police has had a long history of corruption. And when it comes to white police officers interacting with Black citizens, the corruption is oftentimes excused, ignored or covered up. Recently, several stories have come out about corrupt cops in Chicago and their racial attacks on Melanoid citizens.

The city of Chicago recently had to pay reparations to Black torture victims who suffered at the hands of police officers.

So if white police officers have had a history of terrorizing and killing innocent Black people openly, and in many cases, doing it with impunity, is it implausible to believe that law enforcement could also be behind many of the reported shootings that we hear so much of in Chicago?

A few years ago Illinois State Rep. Monique Davis publicly reported that she had heard rumors in the community that police officers were behind many of the reported shootings that were blamed on gang members in Chicago. After she went public with these allegations, she was swiftly criticized by many law enforcement officials and conservative pundits.

"Are Cops In Chicago Behind Many Of The Shootings That Are Blamed On Gang Violence?" The Melanoid Nation Foundation, May 27, 2015.

United Kingdom residents who were in groups that experienced discrimination were less likely to have a positive response, with just over half (53.3%) agreeing or strongly agreeing with the sentiment versus 70.7% of non-discrimination suffering groups.[63] In Norway there were similar gaps between members of the relatively small group that suffered discrimination and those who were not in such groups;[64] though Norwegians overall expressed greater trust in the police and courts than residents of the United Kingdom.[65]

Several Canadian provinces have developed independent agencies to investigate potential criminal conduct by police officers. Ontario's Special Investigations Unit (SIU) was formed in 1990 and was the first such agency in Canada.[66] It is a civilian law enforcement agency with jurisdiction to investigate criminal allegations against police officers and incidents resulting in death or serious bodily injury involving the province's fifty-seven police services.[67] It has a staff of eighty-five and its own forensic investigators, vehicles, and laboratory.[68] The impetus for the formation of SIU was the conclusion reached by the province's general public that "internal investigations lacked the necessary objectivity required of policing."[69] Recommendations to charge officers are made to the Crown Prosecution Service. In 1999, following repeated challenges by police services and officers reluctant to cooperate with SIU, the Police Services Act[70] was updated with regulations that require the cooperation of officers.[71] The Act also requires that police chiefs secure officer-involved crime scenes and immediately notify SIU of incidents that fall within the SIU's mandate as lead investigator.[72] As a result of SIU investigations, charges were laid against fourteen officers in Ontario in 2014 for alleged criminal conduct; four of the incidents were for assaults causing bodily harm or assault with a weapon.[73]

Independent investigative bodies must exhibit a number of common characteristics to be effective. First and foremost is the ability to investigate potential criminal wrongdoing by officers and to make recommendations for prosecutions that are then evaluated by special prosecutors.[74] The independent investigative agency should be open and transparent, independent of any other law enforcement agency, but with unrestricted access to officers and agency records.[75] It must be given a sufficient budget, the power to issue subpoenas, search warrants and a well-defined jurisdiction and mandate.[76] Investigators should be granted all the powers of peace officers.[77]

These characteristics should represent the baseline requirements for independent investigative and prosecuting agencies. Remaining details should be left to state legislatures, especially in light of size differences among states and relative capacity of states' attorneys general to administer such offices. The examples of Northern Ireland, Norway, and Canada should serve as guides for state legislatures in constructing such agencies even though the United States Constitution, unlike the European Convention on Human Rights—of which both the United Kingdom and Norway are signatories—does not impose a duty on states to adequately investigate police-related deaths. Both the United Kingdom and Norway are subject to Article 2 of the Convention, which limits the state's taking of life through "the use of force which is no more than absolutely necessary."[78] In fulfilling the requirements of Article 2, signatory states are inferred to have a duty to ensure "adequate effective investigation of deaths."[79] Even without such a mandate, states should pursue new ways to independently investigate and prosecute deadly uses of force.[80] States' adoption of independent agencies that investigate and prosecute police misconduct would clearly improve upon our current system. First, having independent agencies investigate incidents of possible police misconduct would enhance the truth-seeking process. Independent agency investigators would more likely be free of the institutional allegiances and biases that currently color investigations because they would not feel an impulse to protect fellow members of their own organization. Second, these independent agencies would serve an important expressive function that would likely bolster public trust in our institutions of justice. If the public knows that police-involved deaths are investigated and prosecuted by agencies without close ties to police departments, it will likely have more confidence in the results of those proceedings.

Police departments and local prosecutors will likely strongly object to losing control of these sensitive investigations. It should be apparent to legislatures and other stakeholders, though, that the benefits of thorough and unbiased investigations easily outweigh such notions of territorialism. The result will be greater trust in the process and increased legitimacy of the criminal justice system in the eyes of the public.

Notes

1. See, e.g., Layla Skinns, The Role of the Law in Policing, 2012 J. Police Stud. 225, 234.

2. Melanne A. Civic & Michael Miklaucic, Introduction, The State and the Use of Force: Monopoly and Legitimacy, in Monopoly of Force at xv, xvi (Melanne A. Civic & Michael Miklaucic eds., 2011) (emphasis added).

3. See Sean McFate, There's a New Sheriff in Town: DDR–SSR and the Monopoly of Force, in Monopoly of Force, supra note 2, at 213, 213.

4. See Mike Hough et al., Procedural Justice, Trust, and Institutional Legitimacy, 4 Policing 203 (2010).

5. Kami Chavis Simmons, New Governance and the "New Paradigm" of Police Accountability: A Democratic Approach to Police Reform, 59 Cath. U. L. Rev. 373, 388 (2010).

6. Charles F. Sabel & William H. Simon, Due Process of Administration: The Problem of Police Accountability 27–29 (Columbia Law Sch. Pub. Law & Legal Theory Working Paper Grp., Paper No. 14-420, 2014), http://ssrn.com/abstract=2507280 [http://perma.cc/3Z2P-LNWP].

7. Id. at 30.

8. N.Y.C. Civilian Complaint Revew Bd., 2013 Report 8 (2014), http://www.nyc.gov/html/ccrb/downloads/pdf/CCRB%20Annual_2013.pdf [http://perma.cc/M37N-L5BR].

9. Id.

10. Id. at 6.

11. See Public Comment, Vincent Warren, Exec. Dir., Center for Constitutional Rights, Building Trust and Legitimacy: Listening Session Before the President's Task Force on 21st Century Policing 3–4 (Jan. 9, 2015), http://www.ccrjustice.org/files/CCRTestimony_PolicingTaskforce_20150113Final.pdf.

12. See, e.g., Peter Holley, Ferguson Prosecutor Says He Knew Some Witnesses Were "Clearly Not Telling the Truth." They Testified Anyway., Wash. Post (Dec. 20, 2014), http://www.washingtonpost.com/news/post-nation/wp/2014/12/20/ferguson-prosecutor-says-he-knew-some-witnesses-were-clearly-not-telling-the-truth-they-testified-anyway [http://perma.cc/A94U-V9GJ].

13. Stark Racial Divisions in Reactions to Ferguson Police Shooting, Pew Research Ctr. 2 (Aug. 18, 2014), http://www.people-press.org/files/2014/08/8-18-14-Ferguson-Release.pdf [http://perma.cc/9KZ7-8QPN].

14. Peter Moore, Poll Results: Police, YouGov 2 (Aug. 14, 2014, 11:35 AM), http://cdn.yougov.com/cumulus_uploads/document/vl0h3on24q/tabs_OPI_police_force_20140814.pdf [http://perma.cc/H3AK-3HQE].

15. See Hough et al., supra note 4.

16. Id. at 205.

17. See Jack Sullivan, Clearing the Cops: Do District Attorneys Rubber-Stamp Police Use of Deadly Force?, CommonWealth Mag., Winter 2014, at 29, 36, http://massinc.wpengine.netdna-cdn.com/wp-content/uploads/sites/2/2014/08/CommonWealth_Winter2014.pdf [http://perma.cc/R4AM-WK3W].

18. Scott J. Shapiro, What is the Rule of Recognition (and Does it Exist)? 17 (Yale Law Sch. Pub. Law & Legal Theory Research Paper Series, Research Paper No. 181, 2009), http://papers.ssrn.com/sol3/papers.cfm?abstract_id=1304645 [http://perma.cc/KC77-P7LE].

19. See, e.g., 3 L.A. Police Dep't, 2014 1st Quarter Manual § 794.14 (2014), http://www.lapdonline.org/lapd_manual/volume_3.htm#794 [http://perma.cc/2Q3W-2YDC] (describing that Los Angeles Police Department use of force and in-custody deaths are investigated by the Criminal Investigation Section of the Force Investigation Division).

20. Sullivan, supra note 17, at 30.

21. Id.

22. See Garrity v. New Jersey, 385 U.S. 493, 500 (1967).

23. Merrick Bobb, Civilian Oversight of the Police in the United States, 22 St. Louis U. Pub. L. Rev. 151, 156 (2003).

24. Id.

25. Erwin Chemerinsky, The Role of Prosecutors in Dealing with Police Abuse: The Lessons of Los Angeles, 8 Va. J. Soc. Pol'y & L. 305, 322 (2001).

26. See generally Dan M. Kahan, The Supreme Court, 2010 Term—Foreword: Neutral Principles, Motivated Cognition, and Some Problems for Constitutional Law, 125 Harv. L. Rev. 1 (2011).

27. Don A. Moore et al., Conflict of Interest and the Intrusion of Bias, 5 Judgment & Decision Making 37, 46 (2010).

28. Id. at 47.

29. Chemerinsky, supra note 25, at 315.

30. Id. at 315 n.57 (quoting H. Richard Uviller, The Neutral Prosecutor: The Obligation of Dispassion in a Passionate Pursuit, 68 Fordham L. Rev. 1695, 1702 (2000)) .

31. Id. at 315.

32. John V. Jacobi, Prosecuting Police Misconduct, 2000 Wis. L. Rev. 789, 804 (quoting Alexa P. Freeman, Unscheduled Departures: The Circumvention of Just Sentencing for Police Brutality, 47 Hastings L.J. 677, 719 (1996)).

33. Id. at 789.

34. 42 U.S.C. § 14141(a) (2012).

35. Barbara E. Armacost, Organizational Culture and Police Misconduct, 72 Geo. Wash. L. Rev. 453, 527 (2004) (quoting H.R. Rep. No. 102-242, at 135 (1991)).

36. Addressing Police Misconduct Laws Enforced by the Department of Justice, U.S. Dep't of Justice, http://www.justice.gov/crt/about/spl/documents/polmis.php (last visited Mar. 28, 2015) [http://perma.cc/PV34-JXSP].

37. See Civil Rights Division Special Litigation Section Cases and Matters, U.S. Dep't of Justice, http://www.justice.gov/crt/about/spl/findsettle.php#police (last visited Mar. 28, 2015) [http://perma.cc/T2W5-CGN6].

38. Bureau of Justice Statistics, U.S. Dep't of Justice, NCJ No. 233982, Census of State and Local Law Enforcement Agencies, 2008, at 2 (2011), http://www.bjs.gov/content/pub/pdf/csllea08.pdf [http://perma.cc/6623-9QG4].

39. Stephen Rushin, Federal Enforcement of Police Reform, 82 Fordham L. Rev. 3189, 3193 (2014).

40. Rachel A. Harmon, Promoting Civil Rights Through Proactive Policing Reform, 62 Stan. L. Rev. 1, 1 (2009).

41. See Monell v. Dep't of Soc. Servs., 436 U.S. 658, 694 (1978).

42. No. 3:12cv471, 2013 U.S. Dist. LEXIS 38085 (E.D. Va. Mar. 19, 2013).

43. Id. at *23–24.

44. Id. (quoting City of Canton v. Harris, 489 U.S. 378, 390 n.10 (1989)) (internal quotation mark omitted).

45. Walker v. Sheahan, 526 F.3d 973, 977 (7th Cir. 2008).

46. See, e.g., Rizzo v. Goode, 423 U.S. 362, 378–79 (1976).

47. 461 U.S. 95 (1983).

48. See id. at 105–06; see also Armacost, supra note 35, at 492.

49. See Rushin, supra note 39, at 3193.

50. Police (Northern Ireland) Act, 1998, c. 32 (U.K.).

51. David MacAlister, Final Report, Police-Involved Deaths: The Failure of Self-Investigation, B.C. Civil Liberties Ass'n 40 (2010), http://bccla.org/wp-content/uploads/2012/05/20101123-McAllister-Report-Police-Involved-Deaths-The-Failure-of-Self-Investigation.pdf [http://perma.cc/UQ79-586P].

52. Id.

53. Id.; see Police (Northern Ireland) Act, 1998, c. 32, §§ 50, 54 (U.K.).

54. Police (Northern Ireland) Act, 1998, c. 32, §§ 58–59 (U.K.).

55. 5 Mar. 2004 nr. 13 (Nor.); see also Norwegian Bureau for the Investigation of Police Affairs, Annual Report '09, at 30 (2009), http://www.spesialenheten.no/Portals/0/%C3%85rsrapporter/Spesialenheten_%C3%85rsrapport%2009%20LOW%20-%20engelsk.pdf [http://perma.cc/Z8FD-NWFD].

56. The Norwegian Police—Use of Force (Physically), Norwegian State Response to Christof Heyns, U.N. Special Rapporteur on Extrajudicial, Summary, or Arbitrary Executions, http://www.icla.up.ac.za/images/un/use-of-force/western-europe-others/Norway/State%20Response.pdf (last visited Mar. 23, 2015) [http://perma.cc/M5XG-769P].

57. Id. at 2.

58. Id.

59. Id.

60. European Social Survey, Trust in Justice: Topline Results from Round 5 of the European Social Survey, ESS Topline Results Series Issue 1, at 3 (2011), http://www.europeansocialsurvey.org/docs/findings/ESS5_toplines_issue_1_trust_in_justice.pdf [http://perma.cc/QR23-WRXY].

61. Id.

62. Detailed cross-tabulation data may be accessed via the ESS' online analysis function. See Justice (ESS5 2010), European Social Survey, http://www.europeansocialsurvey.org/data/themes.html?t=justice (last visited Mar. 28, 2015) [http://perma.cc/A6VQ-WQ65].

63. Id.

64. Of the subset of groups in Norway that had experienced discrimination, 75.6% believed the police often made fair and impartial decisions. In contrast, 84.0% of those who did not identify as belonging to a discriminated-against group agreed with the sentiment that police made fair and impartial decisions. Id.

65. See id. (finding that 81.8% of U.K. respondents and 83.6% of Norwegian respondents believed that "police make fair, impartial decisions" "often" or "very often" and that 66.6% of U.K. respondents and 78.5% of Norwegian respondents believed that "courts make fair, impartial decisions based on the evidence available to them" more often than not).

66. See MacAlister, supra note 51, at 44. Other Canadian provinces that have since adopted independent investigative bodies include Alberta, Manitoba, Nova Scotia, and Saskatchewan. Id. at 46.

67. What We Do, Ont. Special Investigations Unit, http://www.siu.on.ca/en/what_we_do.php (last visited Mar. 23, 2015) [http://perma.cc/C4SH-Y2W7].

68. Organizational Chart, Ont. Special Investigations Unit, http://www.siu.on.ca/en/org_chart.php (last visited Mar. 23, 2015) [http://perma.cc/VBN2-W3SA].

69. Ont. Special Investigations Unit, supra note 67; see also Police Services Act, R.S.O. 1990, c. P.15, § 113 (Can.).

70. Police Services Act, R.S.O. 1990, c. P.15, § 113 (Can.).

71. See Conduct and Duties of Police Officers Respecting Investigations by the Special Investigations Unit, O. Reg. 267/10, § 11(3) (Can.).

72. See id. §§ 3–4.

73. See 2014 News Releases, Ont. Special Investigations Unit, http://www.siu.on.ca/en/news.php?yr=2014 [http://perma.cc/E6AE-L5J5].

74. MacAlister, supra note 51, at 72.

75. Id. at 72–73, 76.

76. Id. at 74–76.

77. Id. at 75.

78. Convention for the Protection of Human Rights and Fundamental Freedoms art. 2.2, Nov. 4, 1950, 213 U.N.T.S. 221.

79. Juliet Chevalier-Watts, Effective Investigations Under Article 2 of the European Convention on Human Rights: Securing the Right to Life or an Onerous Burden on a State?, 21 Eur. J. Int'l L. 701, 702 (2010).

80. See Simmons, supra note 5, at 404–08.

> *"Blue Lives Matter and Black Lives Matter agree on one thing: one of the goals of police in the United States seems to be to control black people through the use of violence. The problem is Blue Lives Matter defends this as a good thing."*

Blue Lives Matter Paints Cops As Victims

Adam Quinn

In the following viewpoint, Adam Quinn argues that the "Blue Lives Matter" hashtag—an obvious reaction to the Black Lives Matter movement—perpetuates police violence. Far from a peaceful call to protect police lives, the author contends, Blue Lives Matter fosters an environment of fear, hatred, and racism. The supporters of Blue Lives Matter see cops who kill as victims under attack-turned heroes saving us from the villains, i.e. black "murderers" and "thugs." This dichotomy doesn't allow for any variance, nor does it allow for anything in between. In addition, the author contends, the data does not support that interpretation. Quinn is a historian who has written on anarchism and police.

As you read, consider the following questions:

1. What were the reactions to the video the author describes in the viewpoint?
2. Who were the officers killed in possible revenge for the deaths of Mike Brown and Eric Garner?
3. What is the murder rate for police officers, as cited in this viewpoint?

In the aftermath of the recent killings of Terence Crutcher in Tulsa and Keith Lamont Scott in Charlotte at the hands of police, the Blue Lives Matter hashtag rallied around a video of a group of black youth attacking a white man and taking his pants off in a parking garage in Charlotte. The caption that the most popular Blue Lives Matter twitter account provided for the video reads, "What happens when your POTUS hates the police and when his ideal sons represent Trayvon Martin." It is worth noting that you can't make out anyone's faces in this video—by "representing Trayvon Martin" they don't mean they look particularly similar to him, but that Trayvon Martin, Black Lives Matter protesters, and perhaps black men in general are all violent and brutal. Or, as one reply to the tweet put it, they are "f---ing thugs [who] deserve whatever bad s--- that happens to them."

Other replies to the video include "Animal behavior!" "what a cowardly reprehensible race of ppl," and "and Dems want gun control—SMH." Reactions like these seem to be exactly what the decontextualized video is going for. Though the behavior displayed in the video is far from life-threatening, it's all the validation that Blue Lives Matter needs for its own narrative of the current controversy over police violence: the media is vilifying police officers while the real problem is black violence.

To the Blue Lives Matter crowd, police aren't to blame for killings, rather they should be thanked for defending the white public from thugs like those depicted in the video, who could, apparently, strike at any moment. At least Blue Lives Matter and

Black Lives Matter agree on one thing: one of the goals of police in the United States seems to be to control black people through the use of violence. The problem is Blue Lives Matter defends this as a good thing.

Blue Lives Matter began on December 20, 2014. Their own account of their beginnings is a good summary of their views of current events:

> On August 9, 2014, Ferguson PD Officer Darren Wilson was doing his job as he stopped Michael Brown, who had just committed a robbery of a local convenience store. Brown attacked Officer Wilson in an aggravated assault. Officer Wilson was forced to defend his life by shooting Brown. In the months that followed, agitators spread outright lies and distortions of the truth about Officer Wilson and all police officers. The media catered to movements such as Black Lives Matter, whose goal was the vilification of law enforcement. Criminals who rioted and victimized innocent citizens were further given legitimacy by the media as "protesters." America watched as criminals destroyed property, and assaulted and murdered innocent people, and they labeled these criminals as victims. Personal responsibility for one's actions went away, replaced by accusations of racism and an unjust government.

According to this narrative, it seems as though all those killed by police are personally responsible for their own actions, and are falsely "labeled as victims" after they assault and murder people. Ironically enough, framing it this way is a bald-faced attempt to make "personal responsibility for one's actions" go away for police by presenting killers like Darren Wilson as the true victims.

And some police are victims. Blue Lives Matter's history of their early days continues with a brief mention of Officers Rafael Ramos and Wenjian Liu, who were killed in December 2014 by someone who seems to have been seeking revenge for the deaths of Mike Brown and Eric Garner. However, the organization's narrative quickly moves away from Officers Ramos and Liu and back to Darren Wilson, concluding with, "The officers who founded this organization were motivated by the heroic actions of Officer Darren Wilson, and many others, and decided to create this organization in the hopes that it could prevent more officers from being hurt."

This celebration of actions like Darren Wilson's killing of Michael Brown as "heroic" is a central aspect of the Blue Lives Matter movement. For example, there has been an outpouring of support for Betty Shelby, who shot and killed Terence Crutcher. This is not just a cultural phenomenon but an institutional one; Daniel Pantaleo, who choked and killed Eric Garner, saw a pay raise to $120,000-per-year afterwards. The message being sent to many police is that, if they kill an unarmed person, they either simply get praised by their peers and employers or become a celebrated martyr like Darren Wilson.

Of course, to present people like Darren Wilson as heroes, their victims must be presented as villains. This is where the rhetoric surrounding the tweeted video from Charlotte becomes so crucial to Blue Lives Matter's core message. If shooters like Darren Wilson are actually victims and heroes, and the people they shoot are the true villains, then each and every time police shoot someone, it is another example of police on the defense in a nationwide war on them by predominately black aggressors.

While it might make for a provoking narrative, the idea that police, and not black people, are the ones under attack is not supported by data. As Dr. GS Potter notes in The Huffington Post, the murder rate for the general population in the US is 5.6 per 100,00. For firefighters and EMTs, it is 6.1 and 7.0 per 100,000 respectively. For police, the murder rate is just 4 per 100,000. Even when considering more causes of death than just murder (a police officer is more likely to be killed in a traffic accident, for example, than by gunfire), police officer remains far from the most dangerous job in the US, with fatal injury rates significantly below those of professions like logging worker, fisher, pilot, roofer, and refuse collector.

To put it more simply, in 2015, 42 police were shot and killed in the line of duty. Meanwhile, 990 people were fatally shot by police in the same year. Even the most basic message of Blue Lives Matter requires a complete disregard for reality.

Through their inversion of the truth, Blue Lives Matter is not calling for respect and peace, but for fear. It is in this environment of fear that the rate of police shootings have remained unhindered, continuing roughly at the same rate as in 2015 (of course, there was no consistent data being collected prior to Black Lives Matter's beginnings in 2014).

This remarkably unchanged data may come as a slight surprise considering the efforts made by many communities (and at least some city governments and police departments) to prevent police shootings since 2014. However, on a national scale, the redoubled culture of fear and racism among police outweighs whatever minor reforms that have been put in place so far.

Blue Lives Matter focuses on more than just police, but it always comes back to the core theme of xenophobia and fear-mongering. For example, one of the most-talked about topics on the most popular Blue Lives Matter twitter account and the #BlueLivesMatter hashtag is Donald Trump; support for Trump and support for Blue Lives Matter seems to go hand-in-hand. Even the much less popular "BlueLivesMtr" twitter (a more official account of the Blue Lives Matter nonprofit that mostly retweets news articles) has come out in support of the candidate. The connection between Blue Lives Matter and Trump goes beyond a shared conservatism, and actually tells us a lot about the nature of Blue Lives Matter and its rhetoric of fear.

If presenting the violence of black thugs as the real problem wasn't enough, Blue Lives Matter warns of a hodgepodge of looming threats that wouldn't seem out of place on a Glenn Beck conspiracy chalkboard. Much of Blue Lives Matter's refutation of Black Lives Matter does not focus on the issue of police violence at all, instead opting to use conspiracy theories to support a narrative of xenophobia and paranoia. The official Blue Lives Matter website states that, " The Black Lives Matter organization is… a large, organized, well-planned and funded political action group with international outreach extending to Cuba, Northern Ireland, Europe and the Middle East. The BLM is a tentacle of a Marxist, revolutionary Global movement… [with] significant funding sources… from international currency manipulator and convicted criminal George Soros." The same article argues that Black Lives Matter is a "menace" that doesn't actually want to defend black lives, but seeks to kill police and institute an anti-democratic Marxist regime.

Many have argued that Trump's xenophobic rhetoric could incite racist violence, pointing to the rough turns many Trump rallies have already taken. Of course, Trump's racist fear-mongering is hardly new to America, and it didn't take a Trump presidency for racist violence become institutionalized. Blue Lives Matter is the quintessential Trump-era organization, fueled by—and inciting—fear and hatred of marginalized groups.

This is precisely what makes Blue Lives Matter so dangerous. The movement is not merely a conservative counterpoint to Black Lives Matter, but is ammunition for the racial fears that drive police to shoot unarmed black men to begin with.

The slogan Blue Lives Matter, like "All Lives Matter," is criticized for erasing the particularly high rates of police violence against black people. As a movement, however, Blue Lives Matter is more than a distraction from the almost daily acts of violence against black lives that police perpetuate. Their calls to protect "blue lives," along with their defense (and even celebration) of police violence by framing black men as the true aggressors, make police more fearful of any encounter with black people.

The entire purpose of Blue Lives Matter is to present an image of police across the nation as being the ones truly under attack. And with that, the standard excuse for police to kill with impunity, "I feared for my life," becomes an ideology. No longer do police need to see a suspect draw a gun to fear that their life is in danger. They just have to read some tweets.

Periodical and Internet Sources Bibliography

The following articles have been selected to supplement the diverse views presented in this chapter.

Will Greenberg "Here's how badly police violence had divided America," Mother Jones, March 19, 2017. http://www. motherjones.com/media/2017/03/police-shootings-black-lives-matter-history-timeline-1/

Rory Kramer "Black lives and police tactics matter," Context, October 4, 2017. https://contexts.org/articles/black-lives-and-police-tactics-matter/

Robert Maranto The trouble with police, and Black Lives Matter," *Washington Examiner*, May 11, 2017. http://www. washingtonexaminer.com/the-trouble-with-police-and-black-lives-matter/article/2622735

Joshua Muravchik "The truth about Black Lives Matter," Commentary Magazine, November 16, 2016. https://www. commentarymagazine.com/articles/the-truth-about-black-lives-matter/

Jamilah Pitts "Why teaching Black Lives Matter matters," Teaching Tolerance, Summer 2017, Issue 56. https://www.tolerance.org/magazine/summer-2017/why-teaching-black-lives-matter-matters-part-i

David Smith "The backlash against Black Lives Matter is just more evidence of injustice," The Conversation, October 31, 2017. http://theconversation.com/the-backlash-against-black-lives-matter-is-just-more-evidence-of-injustice-85587

Transforming the System "Racial divide in attitudes towards the police." https://transformingthesystem.org/criminal-justice-policy-solutions/public-opinion-report-a-new-sensibility/racial-divide-in-attitudes-towards-the-police/

Deena Zaru "T.I. speaks out on police brutality," CNN Politics, August 14, 2017. http://www.cnn.com/2017/04/24/politics/ti-us-or-else-movie-police-brutality/index.html

For Further Discussion

Chapter 1

1. Anthony Bradley cites religious teachings as a defense of Black Lives Matter. Should Christianity enter into any arguments in favor of BLM? If so, how?
2. Some people assert that the educational system should teach civil disobedience. Do you believe that should be taught in schools? Why or why not?
3. John Metta points out that only one-third of all African Americans and 12 percent of all American whites understand the goals of Black Lives Matter. What should BLM's leaders do to change those goals or make them better understood?

Chapter 2

1. Leroy Barber contends that Black Lives Matter is more than a one-issue movement. Does he argue his point successfully?
2. Derryck Green asserts that Black Lives Matter should concern itself more with black-on-black crime in inner cities. Should that be the greater focus? Why or why not?
3. How can Black Lives Matter expand its advocacy beyond police reform?

Chapter 3

1. James Simpson argues that Communism is behind the Black Lives Matter movement. Does he offer convincing evidence?
2. How does Melanie Schmitz separate the tactics and motivations of Black Lives matter and white supremacists in asserting that should not be compared?
3. Is Nisa Dang too militant and radical in her claims in favor of BLM activities on the campus of the University of California-Berkeley?

Chapter 4

1. Does Roseanna Sommers conclude that putting body cameras on police officers would reduce the number of violent confrontations with citizens or does she leave that up to the reader? Which passages support your answer?
2. David French claims that the Black Lives Matter movement is based on lies. Does he make valid points? Why or why not?
3. What points does Adam Quinn make in arguing that Blue Lives Matter is doing more harm than good?

Organizations to Contact

The editors have compiled the following list of organizations concerned with the issues debated in this book. The descriptions are derived from materials provided by the organizations. All have publications or information available for interested readers. The list was compiled on the date of publication of the present volume; the information provided here may change. Be aware that many organizations take several weeks or longer to respond to inquiries, so allow as much time as possible.

American Civil Liberties Union

125 Broad Street 18th Floor, New York, NY 10004
(212) 549-2500
website: www.aclu.org

The civil rights of Americans have been the focus of the American Civil Liberties Union (ACLU) since it was founded in 1920. The organization has publicized it supports for the rights and liberties of Black Lives Matter and has decried the use of violence by law enforcement against all citizens as a violation of the First Amendment.

Black Alliance for Just Immigration

1425 4th Avenue, Suite 900, Seattle, WA 98101
(510) 663-2254
website: www.blackallliance.org

Black Alliance for Just Immigration (BAJI) fights for racial justice and immigrant rights. It engages in issue education, advocacy and cross-cultural alliances to help end racism, criminalization, and economic inequality that weakens African-American and black immigrant communities.

Black Organizing for Leadership and Dignity

1001 Connecticut Avenue SW, Suite 201, Washington, D.C. 20036
(305) 590-8224
website: http://boldorganizing.org/

Black Organizing for Leadership and Dignity (BOLD) is a national leadership training program seeking to strengthen the social justice infrastructure for African-American, Caribbean, African, and Afro-Latino citizens and organize their communities more effectively.

Black Youth Project 100

5733 South University Avenue, Chicago, IL 60637
email: http://byp100.org/contact/
website: email: http://byp100.org

The Black Youth Project 100 is affiliated with the Agenda to Build Black Futures, a policy-driving organization that seeks to energize and organize youth in their local communities while stabilizing and revitalizing those communities and honoring the rights of black workers.

Color of Change

5111 Telegraph Avenue, Suite 313, Oakland, CA 94618
email: www.colorofchange.org/contact/
website: www.colorofchange.org

Color of Change works to help people respond to injustice. The online organization toils to move decision makers in the corporate and government realms to create a more humane and less hostile world for black people and other Americans until justice and equality have been achieved.

National Action Network

106 West 145th Street, Harlem, New York 10039
(212) 699-3070
website: www.naacp.org

The National Action Network, which boasts chapters throughout the United States, works to promote a modern civil rights agenda that includes equal opportunities for all people regardless of race, religion, nationality, or gender. Its embraces the spirit and tradition set forth by civil rights movement leader Dr. Martin Luther King.

National Association for the Advancement of Colored People (NAACP)

4805 Mount Hope Drive, Baltimore, MD 21215
(877) 622-2798
website: http://nationalactionnetwork.net

The NAACP has been among the leading advocates for African-Americans for more than a century. Its mission is to seek political, educational, social, and economic equality for all people and eliminate race-based discrimination. The organization works within the political system to improve the lives of those it represents.

National Urban League

120 Wall Street, New York, NY 10005
(866) 698-6831
Website: http://nul.iamempowered.com/

The National Urban League, which has been serving inner city communities for more than 100 years, is dedicated to the economic empowerment of their citizens. The advocacy group works to develop local and national programs, as well as affect public policy.

Organization for Black Struggle

1401 Rowan Avenue, St. Louis, MO 63112
(314) 367-5959
website: http://www.obs-stl.org/

Organization for Black Struggle seeks to contribute to the creation of a society free of exploitation and oppression. Its mission is to build a movement that empowers African Americans politically while fighting for economic justice and cultural dignity, particularly for the working class.

The Praxis Project

1001 Connecticut Avenue SW, Suite 201, Washington, D.C. 20036
(202) 234-5921
website: www.thepraxisproject.org/

The Praxis Project is a movement committed to social change through developing fields of work in ways that encourage multi-level, trans-disciplinary learning that relates to various issues throughout the country and the world. It seeks to create healthy environments and improved educational opportunities in black communities.

Project South

1275 Capitol Avenue SW, Atlanta, GA 30315
(404) 622-0602
website: https://projectsouth.org/

Project South is an organization that has strived to create social justice in the American South for more than thirty years. It produces education tools, curriculum, and workshops that support grassroots organizers, educators, and activists. It also seeks to impact policies at the municipal levels.

Bibliography of Books

Abu-Jamal, Mumia. *Have Black Lives Ever Mattered?* San Francisco, CA: City Lights Publishers, 2017.

Balko, Radley. *Rise of the Warrior Cop: The Militarization of America's Police Forces.* New York, NY: PublicAffairs, 2014.

Boone, Wellington. *Black Self-Genocide: What Black Lives Matter Won't Say.* APPTE Publishing, 2016.

Butler, Paul. *Chokehold: Policing Black Men.* New York, NY: The New Press, 2017.

Caldwell, Farai. *Black Lives Matter: A Collection of Short Stories.* Farai Art, 2016.

Davis, Angela Y. *Freedom is a Constant Struggle: Ferguson, Palestine, and the Foundations of a Movement.* Chicago, IL: Haymarket Books, 2016.

Forman, James Jr. *Locking Up Our Own: Crime and Punishment in Black America.* New York, NY: Farrar, Straus and Giroux, 2017.

Hinton, Elizabeth: *From the War on Poverty to the War on Crime: The Making of Mass Incarceration in America.* Cambridge, MA: Harvard University Press, 2016.

Jones, Willie D. *Today's Lesson: Black Lives Matter.* Will the Wordsmith Publications, 2017.

Lebron, Christopher J. *The Making of Black Lives Matter: A Brief History of an Idea.* New York, NY: Oxford University Press, 2017.

Martinelli, Dr. Ron. *The Truth Behind the Black Lives Matter Movement and the War on Police.* Corona, CA: Graphic PrintSource Inc., 2016.

Parks, Peggy J. *The Black Lives Matter Movement.* San Diego, CA: Referencepoint Press, 2017.

Ritchie, Andrea. *Invisible No More: Police Violence Against Black Women and Women of Color.* Boston, MA: Beacon Press, 2017.

Stamper, Norm. *To Protect and Serve: How to Fix America's Police.* New York, NY: Nation Books, 2016.

Taylor, Keeanga-Yamahtta. *From #BlackLivesMatter to Black Liberation.* Chicago, IL: Haymarket Books, 2015.

Whitehead, John W. *Battlefield America: The War on the American People.* New York, NY: SelectBooks, 2015.

Index